The Simple Science of Muscle Growth and Hypertrophy

The Shockingly Simple Truth on How to Build Muscle using the Best Bodybuilding and Strength Training Exercises

Andy Xiong

© **Copyright 2019 by Andy Xiong**

All rights reserved.

The contents of this book may not be reproduced, duplicated or transmitted without direct written permission from the author.

Under no circumstances will any legal responsibility or blame be held against the publisher for any reparation, damages, or monetary loss due to the information herein, either directly or indirectly.

Legal Notice:
This book is copyright protected. This is only for personal use. You cannot amend, distribute, sell, use, quote or paraphrase any part or the content within this book without the consent of the author.

Disclaimer Notice:
Please note the information contained within this document is for educational and entertainment purposes only. Every attempt has been made to provide accurate, up to date and reliable complete information. No warranties of any kind are expressed

or implied. Readers acknowledge that the author is not engaging in the rendering of legal, financial, medical or professional advice. The content of this book has been derived from various sources. Please consult a licensed professional before attempting any techniques outlined in this book.

By reading this document, the reader agrees that under no circumstances is the author responsible for any losses, direct or indirect, which are incurred as a result of the use of information contained within this document, including, but not limited to, —errors, omissions, or inaccuracies.

I would like to dedicate this book to the individuals that initially helped me get started on my fitness journey. Thank you Moobin, Fayzeen, Sammy and Balin for showing me the ropes and for letting me tag along when I was too afraid to go to the gym.

Cover designed by Brian Du
Instagram: @briandudesign
Website: www.briandu.design

This book is available on Audible

www.andyxiong.com/audible/mgh

Also available on Amazon and iTunes.

Are you new to the concept of audiobooks?

Do you love books and literature but never have the time to sit down and read?

What if you can enjoy your favorite reads another way, perhaps while performing mundane tasks?

Audiobooks are a healthy way of structuring boring tasks.

Sex up what isn't sexy; try out audiobooks today!

Audible has the largest library of audiobooks – not for rent, but for you to own.

Contemporary new books, professional production, and quality narration...

Discover why Audible is the most popular audiobook service,

Get this book in audio for FREE with a one-month free trial of Audible

Table of Contents

Table of Contents..viii

Introduction 1

Chapter 1: The Shockingly Simple Truth on How to Build Muscle 11

Part I The Scientific Evidence................................... 31

    Chapter 2: Introduction to Science, Evidence and Practice, and How to Tell Good Research from Bad 33

    Chapter 3: The Science Behind Muscle Hypertrophy and Why Muscle Hypertrophy is Important 43

    Chapter 4: The Science Behind Muscle Hyperplasia and the Principles Behind Intra-Set Stretching 59

    Chapter 5: Principles-Based Training Method, Backed by Science...67

    Chapter 6: The Science Behind Training Frequency 75

    Chapter 7: The Science Behind Rep Ranges and the Principles behind Exercise Selection 81

    Chapter 8: The Science Behind Training Volume, Sets and Rest Intervals....................97

    Chapter 9: The Science and History of Intensity and Load...111

Chapter 10: The Science Behind Periodization and How to Avoid Overtraining 117

Part II The Principle of Consistency, Motivation, Goal Setting and Plateaus 121

Chapter 11: The Importance of Being Motivated Beyond Yourself 123

Chapter 12: The Importance of Setting Proper Goals and Having a Plan 131

Chapter 13: Self-Management Secrets for Success 141

Chapter 14: How to Tackle Plateaus and Stay Motivated 147

Part III Specificity and Exercise Selection 167

Chapter 15: Muscle Groups, Muscle Function, Origin and Insertion Points 169

Chapter 16: Push Muscles – Training the Chest, Triceps and Anterior Deltoids 175

Chapter 17: Pull Muscles – Training the Upper Back, Biceps and Posterior Deltoids 183

Chapter 18: Leg Muscles – Training the Quads, Hamstrings, Glutes and Calves 191

Chapter 19: Other Muscles – Training the Lateral Deltoids, Traps, Abs and Obliques . 199

Conclusion 205

Bonus: Creating Your Own Muscle Building Program in 3 Simple Steps 209

References 227

Introduction

The health and fitness industry is extremely lucrative. As of September 2018, it is worth a whopping $30 billion in the United States alone. And according to Forbes, it has grown at least 3-4% annually for the last 10 years. [1] As with any industry that is worth a great fortune, opportunists flock to it in hopes of making a quick buck.

However, this presents some serious problems. People like you and I – people who are serious about our health, fitness and personal development – end up bombarded with information, usually in the form of advertorials and infomercials, about what works and what doesn't. And that's not even the worst part: Most of what you learn or hear from mainstream media doesn't even come from actual experts in the health and fitness industry, but from expert *salespeople* who have mastered the art of marketing and branding. Real wisdom from real experts, like qualified coaches, athletes and personal trainers, often get lost in all the noise that clutters the industry. And the ones who do get heard often have to mask themselves as marketers and oversell themselves in order to gain a foothold in the marketplace.

But unless you've already spent a ton of time trying out everything there is in the market, you probably won't even realize that most fitness "experts" are actually marketers who are only in it for the cash. And if you *have* spent a ton of time trying out everything there is in the market, you are probably frustrated with the lack of progress you've made and are already very skeptical of the fitness industry. That's fine, and it is totally understandable.

But that's also why I'm here.

As a marketer and fitness enthusiast myself, I want to dispel all the nonsense in the fitness industry and give you the cold hard truth about building muscle so that you too can build your best body.

But why should you trust a stranger like me? I am a part of the fitness industry, after all. Well, it's simple: I've been where you've been, so I've *felt* how you feel.

I'm not one of those marketers who hop from one industry to another in search of gold; I am a fitness enthusiast with a real passion for fitness. But more importantly, I've figured the muscle-building thing out. I've also figured out the real reason why you and so many others out there are struggling to build muscle – because I was once struggling to build muscle too. And this reason, this truth, is *so* simple and *so* obvious that you'll wonder why you've never figured it out in the first place.

And since I am a marketer, I know all the tricks other fitness marketers use to convince you to believe that their product or service is what you need – when it really isn't. And I'll even expose these tricks to you so that you never fall for them again. But know that not all of these marketing tricks are inherently bad: They have their place in marketing and are legitimate strategies in and of themselves. But like any tool, it is how they are used that you should be wary about.

The first marketing strategy that I want you to be wary about is the repackaging and rebranding of old concepts into something that is considered new and revolutionary. If you buy into a "new and revolutionary" way to build muscle, for example, you are usually sold the same concepts presented in a different way. This isn't trickery, and marketers do it all the time. Oftentimes, there is value added. Other times, people have to be sold the same idea in different ways before they can fully grasp it. Think of how hard it is to reinvent the wheel and you can sort of see why it is a fair thing to do.

The problem, though, is when marketers neither reinvent the wheel *nor* build on it or upgrade it. There are actually marketers who steal other people's ideas and training programs and repackage it as their own – without even fully understanding what they stole. Sometimes, they even sell it at a price that is lower than where they got it from, undercutting the person they stole it from. Other times, marketers may present "new and revolutionary" ways to get fit and muscular that just doesn't work.

The result is a market where all the products and services are the same, with the only differentiator being who can market it the best. If you take a look at the fitness industry today, it is pretty evident that this is where the market currently is. In fact, the latest training revolution is probably blood flow restriction training, which is actually a rebranding of occlusion training. And if you dig a litter deeper, you'll find that occlusion training is Dr. Yoshiaki Seto's patented Kaatsu training from 1994! [2]

This isn't to say that everything deemed new and revolutionary is a rip-off, but if being new and revolutionary is its main selling point... it is safe to assume that the person marketing it is primarily a marketer who knows just enough for you to consider him or her an "expert."

Another marketing strategy that is abused in the fitness industry is overselling the benefits of a product or service. You can expect a little bit of overselling in almost any industry, but there is a difference between overselling benefits and selling straight up lies or unrealistic expectations. It should come as no surprise that a lot of the most idealistic bodies in the fitness industry cannot be achieved without the use of steroids or other substances, but for a marketer to claim that their product or service is the missing piece of the puzzle for you to achieve that look is blatantly wrong.

The last marketing strategy that I want to point out is one that is a lot less obvious than the previous two – not because it isn't used as frequently, but because the negative effects it has on the market is not as evident. I'm talking about the strategy of niching down. What is niching down? Consider my book *[Bodyweight Workouts: How to Program for Fast Muscle Growth using Calisthenics Hypertrophy Training](#)*. It is in a very small niche: It is targeted towards calisthenics practitioners who want to build more muscle, in an aesthetic kind of way. I could have written a book targeted towards the calisthenics niche in general; but because of how the book is positioned and the very small niche it belongs to, it actually has few to no competitors despite being in the very crowded fitness industry.

Now niching down is a very legitimate strategy. Almost all new start-ups and businesses *have* to niche down in order to avoid getting slaughtered by the existing competition. The power of niching down lies in finding very specific problems to address. The more specific the problem, the easier it will be to market the product or service. It also lets you come up with better solutions because the solutions themselves will be more tailored towards the niche. But that's also why niching down can cause so much confusion: Specific problems have specific solutions. People need to address the specifics of the problem they are solving instead of presenting their solution as a universal truth or fix.

For example, I have limited ankle mobility. All my peers would present me with stretches for the muscles in the lower leg when, in reality, it was a problem with my talocrural joint. My peers aren't random gym-goers either; most of them are competitive powerlifters, Olympic weightlifters, strength and conditioning coaches or physiotherapists. Yet, everyone somehow assumed that stretching the calves is all you really need to increase ankle mobility. Joint restriction issues don't even come to mind when people think of limited ankle mobility! So, whenever someone has a magic formula in the health and fitness industry, consider what problem and niche it actually addresses.

The Simple Truth to Building Muscle

But what about this "truth" that I am offering? Is it a marketing ploy as well? Well, sort of. I've had to market it in an exciting way, and I probably oversold how exciting it really is. But let me explain why what I'm about to tell you is different.

First off, what you need is *not* something new or revolutionary. Because, let's face it, almost nothing is new in the fitness industry. Concepts that are new to you today have probably been around for decades. And they've been around because they *work*. The human body is biologically the same as it was 2000 years ago, so what worked to build muscle then works now. And if something *hasn't* worked for you, it's because you didn't apply what I'm about to tell you.

Secondly, although I may have oversold how exciting the truth to building muscle is, it really works. I'm not going to say you will end up looking like the guy on the cover, but I'm not here to sell lies either. I'm here to help you become a better version of yourself, and I can't do that by lying to you or giving you unrealistic expectations of what you can achieve. I know for a fact, though, that you *will* become a better version of yourself with what I'm about to tell you. Why? Because what I am about to tell you can be applied outside of the gym and in your everyday life too.

Lastly, if you've read up to this point of the book, you ARE the target of this book. *The solution in this book addresses the problem that the niche you belong to struggles with.* How do I know? Because you're reading books on how to build muscle, which means you are still looking for a method that works.

And that is precisely what the problem is: **You don't understand the difference between methods and principles**. And until you understand the difference, you will never find an evergreen solution to building muscle. In fact, this is the only thing separating you from those guys at the gym who find success with *any* training program and training philosophy.

That's right: You can make any training program or philosophy work for you if you understand the difference between methods and principles. Does this sound too good to be true? Well it's the truth, so read on to discover why and how.

Chapter 1:

The Shockingly Simple Truth on How to Build Muscle

When it comes to building muscle, some people just can't seem to find anything that works for them. And if you're reading this book, you're probably still searching for something that works for *you*. In fact, you probably stumbled across this book when you were looking for resources on how to build more muscle. Or, maybe you were in search of a new training methodology.

Regardless of how you came across this book, this probably wasn't the first time you were looking for new information on muscle growth. You've probably already read a ton of books, performed extensive research on the science of muscle growth and the sport of bodybuilding, and found plenty of training programs backed by science. And maybe the training programs were proven, netting thousands of people positive results.

So, you ran it… to no avail. It didn't work, like every other training program you've tried. In fact, nothing seems to work. It's déjà vu over and over again. And you're probably frustrated, maybe even to the point where you bash said training program on the Internet. But more importantly, you are left confused and feel like you don't know how to build muscle.

But that's precisely why you aren't building any muscle: The fitness industry has you so wrapped up in all the various methods on building muscle that you've completely neglect the principles. They oversell you on something that is "new and revolutionary," claiming it to be backed by a scientific study taken out of context or from a completely irrelevant niche; and you buy it thinking that it will solve your problem. But truth is the fitness industry just sold you another method, when what you need are principles.

But can you really blame the fitness industry? If the fitness industry tackled the problem at hand, it wouldn't be worth $30 billion today. By pumping out new scientific studies, different training philosophies and new training programs, the fitness industry creates an illusion that building muscle is a very complicated problem with no definite solutions. And because your problem ultimately never gets solved, you will spend upwards of thousands of dollars a year trying to discover how to build muscle.

But why doesn't someone in the fitness industry just sell the truth to building muscle? They could probably pocket a ton of cash. Well, the truth isn't sexy. But more importantly, the truth requires shifting the blame onto you – the customer. And no business wants to piss off their customers.

You see, many people today are looking to blame someone or something other than themselves for their own shortcomings, and training programs are the perfect scapegoat for all the blame. If I was like, "Hey, it's not your training program that sucks – it's you," I'd piss off a lot of people. Instead, the fitness industry would rather avoid pissing off their customers by shifting the blame to individual training methods.

Here's the problem though: You will never really get to the core of the problem if all you do is start blaming individual training programs and philosophies for not working. The fitness industry lies to you so that they can monetize you for life, but they also do it because they don't want to hurt your feelings.

But I'll say it: **It's your fault that you're struggling to build muscle**.

You can have the best training program in the world, custom-made and tailored specifically for you by the most expensive coach in the world, and you probably still won't make much progress. Why? Because the problem is *you*, not the program. You've probably wasted enough time reading articles on muscle growth, searching for the next best program, and achieving mediocre results. It's about time you learned the truth.

If you're offended, so be it. But when you accept responsibility for your own shortcomings, it becomes easy to start building muscle. That's because once you start focusing your attention on applying the principles instead of following the methods, you can make *any* training program work for you. So, stop blaming the methods for failing when it is you who is failing the methods.

Methods and Principles

Now then, what exactly are methods and principles and why does it matter when it comes to building muscle? I'd wager that most of you have probably never even heard of methods and principles in the world of bodybuilding, and that's fine. I've never heard of methods and principles until my fourth year of lifting either. Up until then, all I knew were terms like intensity, frequency and volume.

But unlike many bodybuilding and strength training variables, concepts like methods and principles are on higher plane of thinking. First off, let's start off with some definitions.

A method can be defined as a way of doing or achieving something. Methods are usually established and systematic. In the context of fitness, this means that different training philosophies are individual methods of training. Each training program out there is also its very own method of training as well.

A principle, on the other hand, can be defined as a fundamental truth or law. You *must* obey principles in order to achieve *any* goal. When it comes to building muscle, there are *only 2 key principles* that you must obey in order to build muscle: the principle of specificity, and the principle of progressive overload.

Methods are tangible and systematic, whereas principles are abstract. In the context of building muscle, the principle is that you must stress your body with resistance training and the method would be the philosophy and program you approach training with. Even the exercises you do are methods.

So, while the idea (*principle*) of training to get big and strong is simple to grasp, there are millions upon millions of ways (*methods*) to approach training itself. More importantly, regardless of what method, training program or training philosophy you decide to use, you *must* obey the principles for the method to work.

Here is a quote on methods and principles from Emerson that puts this into perspective:

"As to methods there may be a million and then some, but principles are few. The man who grasps principles can successfully select his own methods. The man who tries methods, ignoring principles, is sure to have trouble."

When someone claims a popular training program doesn't work, they've probably failed to apply the principles of muscle growth when running the program. If the program didn't work, it wouldn't have been popular in the first place. In fact, people who claim that programs don't work probably won't see results with any training program because they are ignoring the principles that make programs work in the first place.

Some of you reading this may be able to relate: Think of a time when you and someone else, training partner or not, ran the exact same program but ended up with staggeringly different results. The person who made less than stellar results likely didn't adhere to the principles. If this is you, the fix is simple: You have to see training as something more than just blindly following a program – you have to see it as a vehicle that brings structure for you to apply the principles.

You see, truth is most people already know what to do to build muscle – eat, sleep, train, repeat – but simply fail to do what they know. It's not as complicated as the fitness industry wants you to believe. There is no perfect combination of volume, frequency, intensity and rest intervals for you to build muscle. It's less about doing things perfectly, and more about working hard and *not* doing the wrong things.

Key Principles of Muscle Growth

Earlier, I mentioned the 2 key principles of muscle growth. The 2 key principles are the principle of specificity and the principle of progressive overload. I will explain what these 2 principles mean in more detail so that you can start building muscle.

The **principle of specificity** states that your body adapts to the training that you do. In other words, *if you want bigger muscles you need to train your muscles.* By partaking in strenuous weight training, your muscles adapt by growing so that they can handle said weight more efficiently. Single-joint isolation exercises shift more emphasis onto the muscles, whereas performing multi-joint compound movements will improve your efficiency with the movements and build muscle as a by-product. Thus, isolation exercises are more specific to building muscle than compound exercises are.

If you've been training hard yet still aren't seeing the results you'd expect to see, you are probably neglecting the principle of specificity. This can take shape in many forms – such as performing only squats but then expecting your arms to grow or failing to actually stress the muscle group that you are trying to grow. Know that – regardless of the program or set and rep scheme – if you are not stressing the muscles you are trying to train, you will not make gains. You can do 3x15, 4x12, or even 10x10 and boast about how hard you train, *but your muscles won't grow unless you actually trained your muscles.*

The other key principle of muscle growth, the **principle of progressive overload**, is really a combination of 2 other principles: the principle of overload and the principle of consistency.

The **principle of overload** states that muscles only adapt when there is enough stress to force an adaptation. Too little stress and there is no need for an adaptation to occur. Many strength programs make use of percentages of your 1-rep max (1RM), occupied with specific set and rep schemes, to try and elicit the proper training stress for growth.

The **principle of consistency** states that you must be consistent with your training. In other words, if you don't use your muscles you will lose your muscles. Believe it or not, even *maintaining* a certain level of fitness or musculature requires consistency. But that's not all: If your goal is to grow continually, you are going to have to always be applying both the principle of consistency and the principle of overload in order to avoid plateaus. That's because, as your muscles grow and adapt to the resistance, the training you do will no longer be stimulating enough to induce muscle growth. Thus, heavier loads will be needed to continue eliciting enough stress for muscle growth.

Since the principle of overload and the principle of consistency are so intertwined when it comes to training, I will often refer to the union of the two principles: The principle of progressive overload. Progressive overload simply means *consistently* applying the principle of *overload*, even as you grow bigger and stronger.

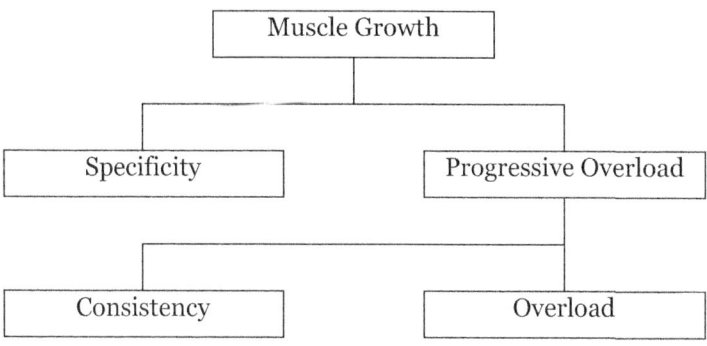

Failure to apply the principle of progressive overload is where I see most regular gym goers mess up. While the person who shows up to the gym once a week is just not consistent enough to make meaningful progress, the gym goers who show up regularly but don't train hard enough to properly apply the principle of overload is the group I really want to focus on in this book. Why? Because nothing's more frustrating than thinking you are making gains only to *not* make gains.

And here's an interesting study: In 2017, 160 recreationally trained gym goers – healthy men who have been training consistently for at least 6 months – were asked to partake in a study. These men were asked to take whatever load they generally used for sets of 10 on the bench press and to perform, in the lab, as many reps as possible with said load under the verbal encouragement of a coach. The results were shocking. When verbally encouraged to give it their all, the participants exceeded even their own expectations: the participants performed, on average, 16 ± 5 reps with a load they normally use for 10 reps! [1] A whopping 13.8% of lifters performed more than 20 reps!

Reps Performed	% of Participants
<10 reps	0%
10-12 reps	22%
13-15 reps	31%
16-18 reps	21%
>18 reps	26%

In other words, most people aren't training hard enough to stimulate muscle growth. Even if the participants were to perform 5 sets of 10 reps with their self-selected loads, a large percentage of them (at least 46%) wouldn't find *any* of the sets challenging.

According to the study people don't push themselves because they don't like the feeling of discomfort. As it turns out, while building muscle is simple, actually training hard is *hard*. And the average lifter is simply not training hard enough to see growth. They're simply not adhering to the principle of overload. That's unfortunate though, because the physiques they're aiming to achieve is most likely *outside* their comfort zone – not inside it.

Key Training Applications

Building muscle was never complicated in the first place. It's as simple as eating more, lifting weights and getting quality rest so that you can recover and adapt to training stress. And then you repeat the process. It's really that simple.

Although most people know what to do when it comes to building muscle, they fail to do what they know because they're not confident in their knowledge. You can thank the fitness industry for praying on your confidence levels by always setting unrealistic expectations and marketing each of the training methods out there as the secret to muscle growth that you need.

Luckily for you, I am a marketer too – and I will present to you the only 2 training applications that, when adhered to, will ensure that you fulfill the principles of specificity and progressive overload!

Firstly, to ensure proper application of the principle of specificity, all you must do is employ proper mind-muscle connection when pumping out reps so that the proper muscles get trained. This often means using lighter weights, performing more isolation exercises, as well as controlling the eccentric portion of each rep (the weight should *never* control you). All these training techniques allow you to focus on using, and ultimately stressing, the muscle(s) that you are aiming to grow.

It's a simple concept, but one that you don't see people apply in the weightroom. It is far more common to see people offload some weight to their joints or use momentum to cheat their reps than to see people employing proper mind-muscle connection.

Next, there are many ways to ensure training is progressive – which would satisfy the principle of progressive overload. But instead of specifically increasing the resistance, the number of reps, the number of sets, or changing the exercise, we can focus on always training hard instead. All the methods of progression do the same thing: Increase the difficulty and training stress in order to avoid and break plateaus. But there's another way to avoid plateaus: *Always train hard, even as you grow in strength and size.*

You can regulate your training so that it is always challenging by taking all your sets to technical failure by performing as-many-reps-as-possible (AMRAP) sets. Stopping at technical failure means ending the set when you know your next rep will be done with dangerous or horrendous form because, let's face it, the very last thing you want to do is risk injury. This means that the number of reps you do will vary by load, by set, and by day. But if you are always pushing yourself to failure you will end up building muscle, regardless of what exercise or load you use.

And here's a bonus: I'll even throw in a third training application that you can implement right now for FREE – because that's what marketers do to boost the perceived value of what they offer. And the third training secret is simple: **Be consistent with your training**.

So, there you have it: mind-muscle connection, AMRAP sets and consistency. These are the tools that will change your life. If you start applying these methods to your training, coupled with good nutrition and good sleep, you should start building muscle *immediately.* These methods are tailored around satisfying the principles of muscle growth, after all.

If you are in awe about how simple muscle growth is, don't be. Nothing should be complicated unless you want it to be. And there is power in simplicity these days because, oftentimes, complexity is why you aren't training as hard as you should in the first place.

So-called experts who try to sell you their overly complicated secrets to building muscle often contradict one another, pulling you in different directions. Even scientific studies, which tackle the fine details of training, are being misinterpreted to be black and white facts. Misinformed evidence-based followers then oversell these findings as fact while completely overlooking the importance of principles. We spend all our time trying to find the magic formula, digging through heaps and piles of information, only to end up forgetting just how important it is to just train hard and to train with specificity in mind. In this day and age, when it is so easy to stumble onto unnecessary information, getting things done is better than doing things perfectly.

Additionally, consider 2 of the most popular and proven strength training programs out there: Starting Strength and StrongLifts 5x5. Both programs are built around a simple principle too: the biological principle of stress, recovery and adaptation (SRA). If these programs can find success in the simplicity of principles, what makes you think simplicity is wrong?

So, while the concepts are easy to understand, know that the execution can be excruciatingly hard. I rarely see people employ proper mind-muscle connection, and the number of times I've seen people train hard or actually take sets to failure is even less. But once you get the execution down, you will start to stand out in your gym. In fact, I guarantee it.

Now that you know the principles of muscle growth, there may be other questions on your mind. Questions like:

- This book is titled "The Simple Science of Muscle Growth and Hypertrophy" but I don't see any science. Is this even backed by science?
- How can I apply the principles of muscle growth to any program so that I can make any method work for me?
- How do training variables – like frequency, volume and intensity – play into this?

- If you take every set to failure, how would you avoid overtraining?
- What about periodization? Isn't periodization important?
- How do I break plateaus?
- Which exercises are best for each muscle group? What exercises do you recommend?

You have probably learned enough to change your life already, so feel free to put this book down and do so. You have the knowledge; now you just need to apply it. But if you are interested in finding out the answers to the questions above... read on because I dedicate the rest of this book to tackling those questions.

ANDY XIONG

Part I

The Scientific Evidence

Chapter 2:

Introduction to Science, Evidence and Practice, and How to Tell Good Research from Bad

Earlier, I brought up the strategy of niching down and mentioned how it is a legitimate strategy for both business and marketing. However, problems occur when people take specific solutions to specific problems and generalize the solution as a universal truth or fix. And believe it or not, it is rampant in the health and fitness industry, especially when scientific evidence is involved.

But first, I want you to be *extra* wary about the claim "backed by science." In fact, the term "backed by science" is as good as useless. Ironic isn't it? Despite how powerful the claim may be, being "scientific" simply means having employed the use of the scientific method, which consists of 5 steps:

observation, hypothesis, experimentation, data analysis, and conclusion. Most of you have used the scientific method before – *in grade school*. The word "scientific" is simply another term for systematic or methodical. If you've ever done adjusted your training program before, such as trying to find an alternate exercise that you can perform without pain, you've trained scientifically!

Yet, when most people hear the term "science," they immediately think of lab coats and Petri dishes – even though science doesn't require any of that. Thus, "science" is not enough: You don't want "backed by science," you want actual research to have taken place: you want "*research-based evidence*".

But here's the problem with research-based evidence: people cherry pick studies all the time. They discuss scientific research that only supports their claim while completely ignoring research that disagrees with it. Yet, *any one study alone is almost never enough to prove a claim*. It's not rare for researchers to come up with different conclusions to the same questions. But of course, different, and sometimes contrasting, conclusions will appear: Each study can be thought of as its own niche. Each study is performed using different methodologies, different researchers with different biases, and completely different subject pools. Therefore, whatever conclusions come up are often specific to the study itself.

That's not to say that scientific research should be ignored, though. The right studies can provide a lot of insight into what is best. You see, there are varying levels of scientific research and evidence. In other words, not all research studies are created equal. Aside from how the study itself was conducted, we can get a gist of how solid a study is through its design. Different study designs include *in vivo* and *in vitro* studies, observational studies, controlled trials, systematic reviews, and meta-analyses.

The Hierarchy of Scientific Evidence

The quality of a study can be most easily determined by its design. Thus, we can quickly determine whether evidence is quality or not based on how the study was designed. For example, some studies are conducted with humans while others are not; some studies are strictly observational with no intervention from the researchers, while others may be controlled; and there even exists reviews that try to gather the results of every study in a field.

Non-human animal studies, also known as **in vivo** studies, are not always the lowest level of scientific evidence available. However, *in vivo* studies are a complicated topic to discuss, mainly because of issues with specificity. Non-human animal studies, for example, can either provide valuable insight in humans or be applicable only to the exact species that they study was conducted on; and often, it falls in the latter. Heck, non-human animal studies may not even be relevant within the same species. Consider domesticated dogs and wolves, both of which are of the same species (Canius lupus) yet require completely different diets. However, sometimes it is unethical or even impossible to perform certain experiments in humans – and that's when non-human *in vivo* studies are most useful. Otherwise, you should steer clear of non-human *in vivo* studies and look only into studies performed with humans.

Studies performed using microorganisms, cells, or biological molecules outside of their normal biological contexts, and often in Petri dishes or test tubes, are called ***in vitro***. Sometimes referred to as "test-tube experiments," *in vitro* studies are sometimes considered the lowest level of scientific evidence. Unlike opinion papers and case studies, *in vitro* studies can be considered scientific because they are systematic and methodical and are based on the methods and principles of science. However, humans differ from test tubes. Heck, test tubes aren't even biological! As such, you should be wary about "backed by science" claims that quote *in vitro* studies.

Cross-sectional studies, case control studies and cohort studies are a step above *in vitro* studies, with each study design being more scientific than the former. However, even these studies themselves aren't good enough for clinical trials because they're all **observational studies**. And there's a good reason they're called observational studies: They're mainly observations, not experiments. Observational studies draw inferences from a sample of a population, meaning the researcher does not actually have control over the subjects that participate in the study. While observational studies are great for identifying correlation, *correlation does not imply* *causation*. For example, 100% of people who have ever drunk water have died or will die, but that doesn't mean that the secret for eternal life is to not drink fluids!

To find causation you *need* experimental data. In fact, the GRADE (Grading of Recommendations Assessment, Development, and Evaluation) approach of assessing whether evidence is of quality or not recommends that any association from observational data be considered to be weak evidence because results from observational studies are, by nature, prone to bias and confounding (meaning having a lurking, but unaccounted for, variable that influences both the dependent and the independent variables) when compared to study designs of higher scientific evidence. Personally, I would stay away from claims backed by observational studies.

Unlike observational studies, researchers involved in **randomized control trials (RCTs)** have control over all test subjects. And when well-blinded, meaning information that may influence results is withheld in order to prevent placebo, randomized control trials are the gold-standard for clinical trials and testing pharmaceutical drugs. But even though randomized control trials are much more scientific than observational studies, they too can sometimes produce contrasting conclusions. And other times, the results of randomized control trials can be swayed through funding or other conflicts of interest. Thankfully, there exists an even higher level of scientific evidence.

At the top of the hierarchy of scientific evidence sits **systematic reviews** and **meta-analyses**. Systematic reviews attempt to combine the results of *multiple* studies in a field of research, which is important because any one individual study – whether controlled or observational – will have flaws. Meta-analyses are systematic reviews with a statistical analysis. Meta-analyses have the added benefit of being a quantitative review, which is favored because numbers are absolute and measurable.

People who try to argue a claim using study designs other than systematic reviews and meta-analyses generally choose individual studies that support their claims, and usually take the results out of context too. In fact, the alkaline diet, as popular as it currently is, was born because of *in vitro* studies showing that cancer cells bred more quickly in acidic environments. Someone took that conclusion and ran with it, but it should be noted that the studies were *in vitro* – meaning it was conducted in a glass dish. To combat the fad, a systematic review published in June 2016 by Dr. Tanis R. Fenton et al. revealed that there is almost no evidence to support the claim that dietary acid and alkaline intake can actually impact your body's pH levels, let alone prevent or treat cancer. [1]

As such, today, research-based evidence is not enough. The alkaline diet was based on research alright, but it's based on *in vitro* research – perhaps the least scientific study design possible. In fact, a ton of supplements in the fitness industry is research-based too, but few have the scientific backing of a systematic review or meta-analysis. That is why there are so few sports supplements that are universally recommended by experts. So, the next time a marketer claims that their training method or supplement is scientifically proven, take a look at the study cited. Oftentimes, reviews will have the words "systematic review" or "meta-analysis" in the title of the study; that's how big of a deal systematic reviews and meta-analyses are in the scientific community. But even then, if you live your life based on whatever research-based evidence shows up next, you'll be jumping bandwagons every time research conclusions change.

Evidence-Based Practice

As stated earlier, research-based evidence is not good enough. Rather, you should shift your focus to *evidence-based practice* instead. Evidence-based practice, pioneered in the medical field by Dr. David Sackett, means embracing uncertainty through "best practices" and experimentation. The premise of evidence-based practice is that science cannot answer all the universe's questions, so it should be used as a starting point for us to create practices that work best for *us*. Evidence-based practice integrates the best scientific evidence, which consists of the most recent systematic reviews and meta-analyses, and your own observations and experiences to deduce what works and what doesn't.

And if you observe how most jacked guys trained, you'd notice that they always train with utmost intensity – which satisfies the principle of overload. And I can guarantee you that they adhere to the other principles of muscle growth too, like specificity and consistency. Why? Because high-intensity training done right almost always equates to muscle and strength. It's evidence-based practice.

In the following chapters I unravel the science behind muscle growth, and then present a principles-based training philosophy backed by the best scientific literature. The principles-based training philosophy is something that you can start integrating immediately, regardless of the training program you are currently running. Then, using primarily systematic reviews, meta-analyses and the highest-quality controlled trials, I explain the science behind how I formulated the principles-based training method – making it evidence-based – and explain how it adheres to the principles of muscle growth. If this interests you, read on.

Chapter 3:

The Science Behind Muscle Hypertrophy and Why Muscle Hypertrophy is Important

People tend to think building muscle is complicated. But when we look at the principles of muscle growth, it doesn't seem that complicated anymore: Train your muscles hard and consistently, and they will grow. But since we covered the how, let's now explore the why: Why do muscles grow when they are trained and stressed?

First, there are only two different ways to grow a muscle. The first of which is muscle hypertrophy, which we will cover in this chapter. The second is muscle hyperplasia, which we explore in the next chapter.

Muscle hypertrophy is the increase in the size of a muscle through an increase in the size of its component cells. It is completely different from muscle hyperplasia, which is the formation of new muscle cells. Depending on your training, muscle hypertrophy may occur through either an increase of contractile proteins or sarcoplasmic volume.

Many stimuli can increase muscle cell volume, the most prominent of which is anaerobic training. These changes happen because of an adaptive response that serves to increase the ability to resist fatigue or generate force in anaerobic conditions. Remember the stress, recovery, adaptation principle that Starting Strength and StrongLifts 5x5 is based off? It's literally that – recovering and adapting to stresses.

However, there are many different biological factors, like nutrition and age, which can also affect the length at which muscle hypertrophy will occur. For example, when males go through puberty, hypertrophy occurs at a much faster rate than before due to a surge in testosterone. Having a good supply of protein and amino acids is also crucial for hypertrophy as they are the building blocks of muscle; hence the importance of eating adequate amounts of protein when your goal is muscle growth.

Since testosterone is a major growth hormone, on average, men find skeletal muscle hypertrophy to be easier to obtain than women. Taking exogenous testosterone, such as anabolic steroids, will increase results. However, anabolic steroids are performance-enhancing drugs, and their use will result in bans or suspensions in many competitive sports. Additionally, testosterone is medically regulated in many countries, which means it is illegal to have without a prescription. Luckily, testosterone levels can rise naturally as a byproduct of weight training, albeit in smaller amounts.

But overall, why muscles grow can be attributed to the simple biological principle of stress, recovery, and adaptation. The question then is: What kind of stress, and how should you train if your goal is muscle growth? But before I answer that, I want to stress the importance of muscle growth in the first place.

More than Vanity

A lot of people believe that muscular strength, muscular size and even muscular endurance define how strong you are. They look at how much weight you can carry, how many pounds you're able to lift, the number of pushups you do, or how big you look. But the relationship between muscular strength, muscular size and muscular endurance is a bit more complicated than that. For now, I want to stress the health benefits that come with muscle growth – particularly the relationship between muscle strength and muscle size.

Muscular strength can be defined as the maximum force a muscle or muscle group can exert when contracted. This is typically measured with a 1-rep max (1RM) test. During this test, a person performs an exercise for one rep at maximal loads to see how much they can lift.

However, there are many factors that can affect how strong you are, how you perform on a 1RM Test, and whether you are strong enough to accomplish your daily exercises and chores. These include muscle size, the different muscle fibers and the ratios at which they exist, your anthropometry (your bone anatomy and segment lengths), variances in your muscle origin and insertion points, and the proficiency of the movement you perform. Of these, you only have full control over movement proficiency and muscle size. [1]

In other words, muscle size is important even for athletes and individuals that aren't interested in competing in bodybuilding shows: bigger muscles generally mean stronger muscles. The two go hand-in-hand. You may see small individuals who can put up a lot of weight on a deadlift due to great movement proficiency – but you cannot deny the fact that if you were bigger than you currently are, you would be stronger than you currently are. The same goes for those individuals; given bigger muscles they would put up *even more* weight on the deadlift.

But even if you're not a strength athlete, powerlifter, or strongman, muscle size and strength is an indicator of one's general health. Muscle atrophy happens when there is a decrease in muscular strength because of a decrease in your muscle mass (in other words, a loss of size or mass in the component cells of the muscle).

This could be complete or partial atrophy, varying by the extent of your muscle weakness. The most severe cases of muscle atrophy are generally caused by health problems like burns, renal failure, chronic obstructive pulmonary disease (COPD), congestive heart failure, AIDS, and cancer. Yet, smaller health issues can also result in muscle atrophy. For example, starvation can also lead to muscle atrophy. A simple disuse of muscles, bad rest, poor movement patterns, or a sedentary lifestyle can also cause atrophy.

Muscle atrophy is partially caused by the normal aging process. When atrophy happens due to aging, it is called sarcopenia. Muscle sarcopenia can be slowed with resistance training. Though there isn't a clear reason as to why it happens, it's believed that the cause of sarcopenia is due to a decrease in the number of satellite cells and its ability to effectively regenerate muscle fibers. I'll talk more about satellite cells in the next chapter, as they play an important role in muscle hyperplasia. But for now, understand that resistance training is crucial for slowing down muscle sarcopenia.

On the other hand, the loss of muscle from reasons other than sarcopenia and atrophy indicates the presence of diseases that result in muscular defects or autoimmune responses that degrade the structure of the muscle. But because muscle growth is based on the principle of stress, recovery and adaptation, training can help prevent these muscular defects: The adaptation to training stress results in an increased resiliency to overall stress.

Now that you understand the importance of resistance training and muscle size, let's go beneath the skin and take a closer look at the strands of muscle fibers in our bodies.

The Two Types of Muscle Fibers (and Why You Need Resistance Training)

Your muscle tissue is a very complex structure complete. Muscle tissue is made up of strands of muscle cells called muscle fibers, which are held in a thick band of connective tissue called perimysium. Of these muscle fibers, there are two different types.

The first type of muscle fibers, also called "slow-twitch" muscle fibers, is rich in myoglobin and mitochondria and dense in capillaries, which means they are resistant to fatigue. On the contrary, they don't have much potential for power output and growth. Slow-twitch muscle fibers are also referred to as Type I muscle fibers.

The second type of muscle fibers, also known as "fast-twitch" muscle fibers, grow more quickly than slow-twitch muscle fibers and contract faster. This means that fast-twitch muscle fibers have a higher power and strength potential. The main "downside" is that they fatigue much faster, which makes them less suited to endurance activities. Fast-twitch muscle fibers are also called Type II muscle fibers.

Different muscles have different amounts and ratios of Type I and II fibers, and there is continuous debate about what causes this distribution. The main question is: Why do some people have more Type I muscle fibers than Type II and vice versa? Genetics likely is the reason why, and it's unlikely we can change one type into another through training alone. Another reason is the function of the muscles themselves: Postural muscles tend to have a higher percentage of Type I muscle fibers in order to maintain proper posture for longer periods of time. For example, the soleus – one of two calf muscles – tend to have a distribution of 90% Type I muscle fibers to 10% Type II muscle fibers, whereas the triceps brachii – a non-structural muscle – is generally the muscle with the highest ratio of Type II to Type I muscle fibers, sitting at an average distribution of 70% Type II to 30% Type I muscle fibers. [2] At the end of the day though, you don't have much control over your distribution of Type I and II muscle fibers. As such, there's no reason to fret over your muscle fiber distribution.

That being said, it is believed that training *can* alter Type II muscle fibers, causing them to change from Type IIb glycolytic (also referred to as Type IIx) to Type IIa oxidative. Type IIa oxidative muscle fibers are a bit more resistant to fatigue, and thus can produce large amounts of force for longer periods of time. Think of Type IIb as strength and Type IIa as power: Like how power is an expression of strength and speed, Type IIa muscle fibers are an expression of the power of Type IIb muscle fibers but for longer periods of time.

Due to their larger power output, Type II muscle fibers tend to respond better to low-rep, high-load training. Type I muscle fibers, on the other hand, tend to respond better to high-rep, low-load training because of their lower power output and higher resilience to fatigue. This explains why heavy weight training is often better than endurance training for muscle building: Type II muscle fibers grow much more quickly and have a higher growth potential than Type I muscle fibers. This means a much more muscular physique in a shorter period of time; hence why individuals who want a more muscular physique pick up dumbbells and barbells and partake in resistance training as opposed to hopping on a treadmill.

The Two Types of Hypertrophy

Large muscles are usually associated with being very strong. While there is a connection between size and strength, having a lot of muscle mass doesn't necessarily mean that you are stronger than someone else with less muscle mass. For example, a powerlifter tends to have more strength than a bodybuilder, but bodybuilders look like they have a lot more muscle mass at similar weight classes. Although you can argue that powerlifters and bodybuilders may compete at different body fat percentages, different body adaptations also occur during their training.

Muscle hypertrophy happens when the myofibrils increase in size. Myofibrils are small muscle fibers in the muscle. Bodybuilders tend to have more non-contractile connective tissue and collagen that contributes to the size of their muscles due to training in ways that encourage *sarcoplasmic hypertrophy*. This gives bodybuilders a more inflated look. Powerlifters and strength athletes train in a way that maximizes *myofibrillar hypertrophy*. Since myofibrillar hypertrophy happens due to the increase of the number of contractile proteins in the muscle fibers, the muscles can produce much more force and have a denser look at low body fat percentages.

Let's cover sarcoplasmic hypertrophy first, since that is what is commonly associated with bodybuilding and, subsequently, muscle growth. Broken down, sarco- means "flesh" and -plasmic refers to plasma, a gel-like material in the cell containing various important particles. Sarcoplasmic hypertrophy is the result of an increase of muscle size due to the increase of fluid volume in the muscle fibers, though increases in other non-contractile components of your muscles are also categorized as sarcoplasmic hypertrophy. Although sarcoplasmic hypertrophy doesn't increase the amount of force you can output, muscle growth through sarcoplasmic hypertrophy does aid in increasing strength by creating shorter moment arms which can result in better leverages for lifting.

When training to increase muscle mass through sarcoplasmic hypertrophy, the goal is to isolate and stress only the muscles you are trying to build in order to achieve a "pump." This generally means that the movements and exercises you do are very inefficient and impractical. Think bodybuilding movements like the triceps extension. The goal is to minimize stress to both your joints and the nervous system, and to put as much stress on the triceps. Personally, I see a lot of people perform triceps extensions incorrectly; when you fully extend your elbows in triceps extensions, a lot of the weight is taken off the triceps and transferred to the joints. In fact, for exercises like triceps extensions, utilizing partial reps and shorter ranges of motion can help with adherence to the principle of overload and the principle of specificity. For more information, go to www.andyxiong.com/bonus/hypertrophy.

Systematic stress, from something like heavy deadlifts, is harder for the body to recover from than isolation movements like the hamstring curl. If you've ever done heavy deadlifts, you'd know that you can end up being fatigued for days. But the more time is spent recovering outside of the gym, the less volume you can accumulate. Volume drives hypertrophy: the more volume you can accumulate, the more gains you make. Single-joint isolation movements, by nature, are easier to recover from, allowing bodybuilders to train much more frequently and with much shorter rest times. Bodybuilders want to accumulate lots of volume in shorter periods of time.

But what about myofibrillar hypertrophy? Myofibrillar hypertrophy refers to a real increase in the number of contractile proteins (actin and myosin) in the muscle fibers. This results in greater outputs of force. In terms of raw strength, you would want to maximize myofibrillar hypertrophy by contracting your muscles hard during the concentric to induce mechanical damage.

When resistance training, you will experience both myofibrillar hypertrophy and sarcoplasmic hypertrophy. Some individuals may favor one over the other, but if muscle growth is your overall goal you should train in ways that stimulate both forms of hypertrophy. (Though, it's not like you can realistically train in such a way that completely isolates one form of hypertrophy from the other.) This means your training should be varied, incorporating compound exercises, isolation exercises, low loads, high loads, low rep ranges, as well as high rep ranges. Thus, even if your goal is bodybuilding, you should not neglect building strength; don't avoid multi-joint strength training compound exercises like the barbell back squat just because you hate squatting!

Note that I did not say that you must *train* like a strength athlete though. All I said was that you should incorporate strength training exercises into your training regime. Some of you may be shocked to hear this, but I'll explain why in Chapter 7. But before that, let me tell you about another way to potentially build *infinite* amounts of muscle: hyperplasia – muscle growth through the development of new muscle fibers. Read on.

Chapter 4:

The Science Behind Muscle Hyperplasia and the Principles Behind Intra-Set Stretching

In the previous chapter, I briefly mentioned muscle hyperplasia. But what is muscle hyperplasia? Muscle hypertrophy is the increase in the *size* of muscles cells, whereas muscle hyperplasia is the increase in the *number* of muscle cells. That would mean that there are potentially three ways to increase muscle mass: myofibrillar hypertrophy, sarcoplasmic hypertrophy, and muscle hyperplasia.

Unfortunately, there is a ceiling to how much you can grow with hypertrophy: Because hypertrophy is the increase of the size of the muscle cells, how much muscle you can build is limited to the number of muscle cells you have. On the other hand, there is no such limit with muscle hyperplasia: You could potentially increase the number of muscle fibers you have indefinitely.

However, whereas muscle hypertrophy is a response to training stress on the muscle fibers, muscle hyperplasia is usually a response to an excess of growth factor, or hormones, in the body. To understand why, we must understand the instances that hyperplasia occurs naturally in the human body.

Hyperplasia naturally occurs in the human body; an example of which is in lactating mothers. When lactating, breast tissue undergoes hyperplasia. When you have an infection in the throat, your tonsils also grow because of hyperplasia. However, whether it is possible to stimulate *muscle* hyperplasia with resistance training is questionable.

Researchers have come up with many ways to force lab animals to undergo resistance training, some of which resulted in muscle hyperplasia. However, there are many studies with contradicting conclusions as well. Although there are some human studies that suggest the occurrence of muscle hyperplasia through resistance training, the most convincing data has always come from non-human animal experimentation. I've stated before that you should be skeptical of *in vivo* studies, but non-human animal studies do have a place in science: If there are logistical or ethical reasons that prevent human research, *in vivo* studies are as good as it gets. But here's the problem: It *is* ethical to perform resistance training studies on humans. As such, *in vivo* studies regarding muscle hyperplasia are as good as useless today. And the records reflect that: Most studies on muscle hyperplasia are from the 1970s.

In fact, muscle hyperplasia is one of those niches that fitness marketers swarm to. This is because of all the available research – mostly *in vivo* studies, all predating the year 2000 – suggesting that there is a way to trigger muscle hyperplasia through resistance training. The *how*, though, is unclear. Yet, marketers take advantage of this by marketing their training method(s) as the *how-to* to inducing muscle hyperplasia, and then cite *in vivo* studies from 3 to 5 decades ago as scientific evidence that muscle hyperplasia is possible through resistance training.

So, whereas muscle hypertrophy has been well documented and accepted, muscle hyperplasia hasn't ever really been measured in humans. In fact, the only meta-analysis done on muscle hyperplasia was published in 1996 by Dr. George Kelley et al., and it wasn't even a study on humans – in fact, it purposely excluded all studies on humans and looked only at non-human mammals and birds. [1] Since the turn of the century, there has been no further research conducted on muscle hyperplasia.

The focus in the scientific fitness community shifted to other things like inter-set stretching, which is simply performing stretches in between training sets. However, in 2017, there were rumors going around that heavy inter-set stretching *can* induce muscle hyperplasia. And the "scientific" evidence that it works? That's right: Non-human animal studies performed between 1960 and 2000. Regardless, more and more people started taking an interest in muscle hyperplasia again, and the scientific community took notice. Research began on muscle hyperplasia and, more specifically, its relationship with inter-set stretching. Overall, results were mixed. While some studies found that inter-set stretching resulted in more muscle growth, others found that it did nothing at all.

Still, there isn't much data on inter-set stretching and hyperplasia. No systematic reviews and meta-analyses on inter-set stretching exist as of the writing of this book. But in July 2019, Dr. Evangelista et al. published a trial where untrained participants that had stretched for 30 seconds in between sets produced twice as much muscle growth than participants who didn't! [2] However, the growth wasn't because of hyperplasia. In fact, if you take a principles approach to understanding inter-set stretching, you will realize that it is nothing new – it's just another method of stimulating muscle growth through *hypertrophy*.

Taking a muscle into a stretched position has been shown to independently increase the activation of signaling pathways associated with muscle hypertrophy. [3] In other words, stretching, like contracting a muscle, results in hypertrophy because stretching results in mechanical tension. In fact, the opposite of contraction isn't elongation but relaxation – and your muscles are far from relaxed when you're stretch. Heck, the Romanian deadlift is literally a loaded stretch for the hamstrings! Thus, because stretching results in hypertrophy, inter-set stretching can be thought of as performing a superset of Romanian deadlifts and hamstring curls. (A superset means performing a set of Romanian deadlifts followed by a set of hamstring curls and repeating, that as opposed to performing sets of only 1 exercise at a time.) And what strategy do you think will result in more muscle growth: A superset of 4 sets of Romanian deadlifts with 4 sets of hamstring curls, or 4 sets of hamstring curls alone?

In other words, inter-set stretching is just another *method* of unknowingly accumulating a LOT more volume. Volume is one of the main drivers of muscle hypertrophy, but because it isn't common practice to count your stretches towards your total volume, people tend to think that the magic is in the method of inter-set stretching itself. But no, the magic is in doing more volume: The magic is in the principle of overload.

Don't start stretching between sets and expect more muscle growth, though. Because inter-set stretching depends on the principle of overload, it's not something that would benefit anyone and everyone. In fact, Dr. Evangelista's trial used untrained lifters, which may explain why only 30 seconds of inter-set stretching made such a profound effect at the end of the study: the stretching likely contributed a lot to the participants' weekly volume, as even light stretching was overloading the previously-sedentary individuals' muscles. But if you're already flexible, light to moderate inter-set stretching probably wouldn't result in the overload that's necessary for muscle growth in the first place.

To this day, proponents of muscle hyperplasia suggest that muscle hyperplasia can still happen, and in one of two ways: 1) Either by splitting the pre-existing fibers, or 2) by activating satellite cells that live around your muscle fibers and hope that they mature into new muscle fibers. But none of these are possible through weight training. Although satellite cells can be changed into new muscle fibers, the most proven, and perhaps only, way to do so is with anabolic steroids. This does mean that steroid users have a permanent advantage over natural athletes though: Even when steroid users cycle off, they have increased potential for muscle growth and performance due to having more muscle fibers.

So, in summary, yes, muscle hyperplasia is possible in humans – but mostly with the use of exogenous hormones. There is no known way to trigger muscle hyperplasia through training alone. Muscle hypertrophy is a much more feasible and proven way to increase muscle size; hence why this book is focused on hypertrophy and not hyperplasia.

That's not to say that inter-set stretching is useless though. It may not stimulate muscle growth through muscle hyperplasia, but as a method it encourages people to overload their muscles. That alone gives merit to its existence. But as you can see, all methods have a place provided that the principles are adhered to. As such, in the next chapter I will present to you a training method, or ideology, that enforces you to adhere to the principles of muscle growth. Keep reading to learn about this principles-based training method.

Chapter 5:

Principles-Based Training Method, Backed by Science

You were introduced to the concept of principles and why principles matter more than methods (like training philosophies and training programs) in the beginning of this book. I then explained how most people fail to tackle the principles yet blame the methods when they fail to build muscle. As a reminder, the 2 key principles you must adhere to for muscle growth to occur are specificity and progressive overload. The principle of progressive overload can be broken down into the principle of consistency and the principle of overload. Fulfill these principles and your muscles will grow, regardless of what method you use to approach the principles. But knowing the principles of muscle growth is not enough. You must be able to *apply* them.

In Chapter 1, I gave you two training applications you can apply – mind-muscle connection and AMRAP sets – that, when combined with consistent training, adequate rest and proper nutrition, should remedy most of the problems you have with building muscle. With these tools, you have a very solid foundation for principles-based training. Better yet, you can use this principles-based training foundation for any training program of your choice, turning any method into one that will work for you. All you must do is turn your prescribed sets into AMRAP sets, and employ better mind-muscle connection when it comes to performing your reps.

And here's the truth when it comes to training methods: There is no specific training method, philosophy or program that is the best. The results of whatever training routine you use will vary depending on the person. And the more you understand and can apply the principles, the better the results you will see.

So, if you are someone who does not understand the principle of overload, the best training program will be the ones that force you to train *hard*. This can be done with pre-programmed AMRAP sets. Other methods of progressively overloading your muscles also work, including inter-set stretching that we went over in the previous chapter. But even with an ideal program, your gains will be dictated by whether *you* take your sets to failure or not. Oftentimes people will cut their sets short of failure and wonder why they don't make gains.

On the other hand, if you are an individual who isn't consistent with your training the best training program will be the one that you adhere to. This could mean something that looks fun, or it could mean *just having a training routine in the first place* so that you have a reason to get your butt in the gym. If you lead a chaotic life, introducing structure to your life through simply having a training program will pay dividends.

Lastly, if you struggle with the principle of specificity, consider employing internal cues like "*mind-muscle connection.*" What are internal cues? Internal cues are cues that focus on a particular part of the body and how it moves or how it feels; in contrast, external cues focus on the outcome of the movement. Not only does the utilization of internal cues increase activation of the target muscle, but it usually results in increased activation of surrounding muscles too – particularly those that act on the same joint as the target muscle (synergist and antagonist muscles). [1][2] As for why internal cues work, it is speculated that consciously focusing on only one particular muscle or muscle group (also known as mind-muscle connection) results in inefficiencies in motor control. You see, when you focus on the outcome of a movement via external cues, your nervous system subconsciously figures out the most efficient way to move. When you shift your focus to internal cues you disrupt your nervous system, resulting in the need for greater muscle activation in order to accomplish the same movement. [3]

But what does science have to say? We've already covered how marketers take advantage of the fitness industry by citing "scientific" studies that are very low on the hierarchy of scientific evidence, and we came to the conclusion that the most trustworthy studies are going to be systematic reviews and meta-analyses. Currently, there are hundreds of systematic reviews and meta-analyses, so science actually has a *lot* to say about optimizing muscle growth through resistance training.

In this chapter, I will quickly lay out evidence-based recommendations for all of the variables involved in programming for muscle growth; the following chapters will explain the research that went about coming to these conclusions.

The first training variable that comes to mind when you approach building muscle is **training frequency**, or how many days you plan on training per week. Generally, a higher training frequency is better, and the lowest frequency I can recommend is 2 days per week. Of course, the best training frequency would be the one that allows you to be the most consistent with your training so that you can satisfy the principle of consistency: There is no point trying to train 6 days a week only for you to give up on the second week of training. I cover the science behind frequency in Chapter 6.

The next variables I want to talk about are **rep ranges** and **exercise selection**. You can probably guess how many reps I want you to perform per set.

Here's a hint: As many reps as possible. *Take your sets to failure.* This is a surefire way for you to adhere to the principle of overload. However, if you are a strength athlete where muscle growth isn't the primary goal, you are an exception; and I'll explain why in Chapter 7. Though I cover exercise selection in Chapter 7 too, I go more in-depth in Part III.

In Chapter 8, we will discuss **volume** and **sets**. You will learn the various methods of calculating volume, as well as the proper way to quantify volume specifically for muscle growth. We will also discuss rest intervals between sets. For now, know that the recommendation is to perform at least 10 sets, taken to failure, for each muscle group that you want to grow, per week.

In Chapter 9, we will talk about **intensity** and **load**. Depending on whether you are a bodybuilder or strength athlete, intensity and load can have the exact same meaning or completely different meanings. As such, we will give the two variables concrete definitions and identify the best training intensities and loads. For now, know that training at higher intensities is better than training at lower intensities.

Finally, Chapter 10 will cover **periodization** and **overtraining**, two things you will likely never have to worry about if your primary goal is muscle growth. Chapter 10 will be a shocker for most of you; as it turns out, periodization doesn't matter for muscle growth!

If you want to see these variables applied to a training program or want to learn how to write your own non-periodized program in 3 simple steps while following these suggestions, I've included a bonus chapter and free complimentary hypertrophy training program at the back as a thank you for purchasing this book.

Whether you are going to create your own muscle hypertrophy program, use the one I give you in the link above, or find an existing training program to modify so that it becomes principles-based, know that the focus of this book is not on doing a "program" but on changing the way you live your life. You see, principles are not a fitness or bodybuilding concept. Principles are applicable to anything in life. If you can shift your focus from methods to principles, you will be a lot more successful in all your endeavors, as you will soon see in Part II of this book. For now, read on to discover why training frequency is perhaps the first, and maybe most important, variable to have figured out.

Chapter 6:

The Science Behind Training Frequency

Almost everyone focuses on training volume, even the researchers who conduct scientific studies. But what if I told you that frequency was equally as important? In this chapter, discover how slightly tweaking your training frequency can result in a *lot* more muscle growth.

But first, what is frequency? It is how often you train or, more specifically, how often you train a movement or muscle group per week. A frequency of 2 for biceps means that you will train biceps twice a week, usually on two separate training days. Now it's true that volume is *the* driving factor for muscle growth. But there also exists a relationship between volume and frequency; meaning frequency is also a driving factor for muscle growth.

You might be wondering what the ideal training frequency is, or how often you should train. Well, the answer is simple: At least twice a week, and up to as often as you want. If you're afraid you'll overtrain, you won't: The inverse relationship between frequency and volume per training session means that you can easily control your levels of stress by maintaining a constant weekly training volume. For example, if you train very frequently, your volume per training session will be a lot lower. If you train infrequently, your volume per training session will be a lot higher. I go more in-depth about this relationship in Chapter 8.

As for the twice a week lower limit, there are two reasons. The first reason, which we will talk about in this chapter, is that it's scientifically proven to be superior than training muscle groups once a week. A systematic review and meta-analysis published in November 2016 by Dr. Brad Schoenfeld et al. revealed that training muscle groups twice a week resulted in significantly more gains – about 63% more – than training muscle groups once a week, when volume was equated. [1] In fact, if you look at the study, the results were truly significant: Not only did it review 10 different studies, but the difference between higher frequency and lower frequency training was an effect size of 0.49 ± 0.08 versus 0.30 ± 0.07 respectively – meaning even the best results from training muscle groups once a week could not compare to the worst results of training muscle groups twice a week! Thus, if you dedicated one day a week to training arms, splitting that over two different training days will guarantee more muscle growth.

However, it's unclear whether higher frequencies will result in even more muscle growth. If we turn towards strength training for answers, it probably wouldn't hurt. Aside from increasing frequency to increase training volume, powerlifters and weightlifters are known to perform their competition lifts multiple times a week. In fact, many weightlifters squat heavy 6x a week – and, sometimes, even multiple times a day! Why? Because high frequency training lets you train fresh and well-rested. Imagine performing 12 sets of biceps curls to failure in one workout, versus performing 4 sets to failure spread out over 3 workouts. In the second scenario, rep quality will be a lot higher, meaning better mind-muscle connection throughout. That in turn results in greater training specificity because you aren't cheating reps – and specificity is a *key* principle for muscle growth.

And contrary to popular belief, *how* you spread out training frequency doesn't seem to matter. A 12-week study published June 2018 by Dr. Yifan Yang et al. found no significant differences in strength gains or body composition changes between participants training thrice weekly on 3 consecutive days and those that trained on non-consecutive days. [2] While it may be better to spread out your training sessions, the benefits from doing so are probably a lot smaller than initially thought. And the benefits are probably even smaller for hypertrophy purposes, as volume is the main driver for hypertrophy. Thus, if your schedule is tight, training twice a week – on weekends only – is sufficient to make gains.

Now look at your previous training. How frequently did you train each muscle group? Do you notice a relationship between the size of your muscles and how frequently you trained them? Now that you know the importance of training frequency, will you continue to train using bro-splits – a training structure where you only train each body part once a week, based on the theory that your muscle groups need a full week to recover? And what about the other training variables? Is there a way to optimize them, too? Read on to find out.

Chapter 7:

The Science Behind Rep Ranges and the Principles behind Exercise Selection

You know those specific rep ranges for strength, hypertrophy, and endurance? It was something along the lines of 3-8 reps for building strength, 8-15 reps for muscle growth and 15+ reps for endurance, right? Well, it doesn't matter because it turns out that they're not too accurate after all: You can build muscle using nearly any rep range!

But first, what is a rep? A repetition, or more commonly referred to as a rep, is the movement of an exercise through its complete range of motion. Consider the barbell bench press: When you are bench pressing, you must lower the barbell until it makes contact with your chest, then you have to press it back up until your arms are fully extended and locked out. Once this has been accomplished, you have done one rep. If you do this action 10 times, you would have completed 10 reps.

Rep ranges don't matter as much as you think it does when it comes to hypertrophy. In fact, the ideal, or golden, rep ranges of 8-12 reps or 6-15 reps are *more for optimizing the old formula of volume than it is for optimizing muscle growth.* But because there is a new and more accepted way of calculating volume for hypertrophy (which we will cover in Chapter 8), those ideal rep ranges aren't ideal anymore – they're just like any other rep range.

You should understand by now that the principles of muscle growth are progressive overload and specificity. You should also understand that if you adhere to these principles, any training method, philosophy, or program will work. Thus, as long as you take your sets to muscular failure on a consistent basis, properly utilizing the muscles you are trying to grow, you can induce muscle hypertrophy with *any* rep range.

But this isn't because a principles approach to training is superior, and it isn't because that's what this book is selling. In fact, it has been proven by science: A systematic review and meta-analysis published in the end of December 2017 by Dr. Brad Schoenfeld et al. revealed that you can indeed build muscle with a variety of rep ranges. The meta-analysis looked at a total of 21 different scientific studies and revealed that, *when performing AMRAP sets or taking sets to failure*, training with loads less than 60% of your 1RM for higher repetitions and training with loads greater than 60% of your 1RM for fewer repetitions resulted in very similar isometric strength gains and muscle hypertrophy. [1] The only difference was that training with heavier loads resulted in greater increases in your 1RM, while training with lighter loads resulted in better adaptations to higher repetition training. Thus, overload being a key principle of muscle growth isn't pseudoscience – it's backed by *real* science, in the form of a meta-analysis.

Many other trials exist to fill the holes of the analysis. For example, a study published by Dr. Sanmy R. Nóbrega et al. in January 2018 found that training with 30% of your 1RM can build just as much muscle as training with 80% of your 1RM – so long as the number of sets was equal, and that you take each set to failure. [2] Failure training isn't a gimmick that has been proven to work only because the people studied were untrained lifters making beginner gains either; it's been proven to be just as effective in well-trained men too. [3]

So then, why spend hours at the gym performing the levels of "volume" you would find in something like German Volume Training when you can stress the muscle just as much in less time and with less repetitions? Your muscles don't know that 10x10 is twice the "volume" or repetitions that 5x10 produce. Your muscles only respond to the stress it goes through. It doesn't know that 20+ reps are for endurance or that 8-12 reps is the ideal rep range for muscle growth; nor does it understand that your set of 3 reps is for raw strength. These are just observations that *try* to explain the relationship between different rep ranges and muscle adaptations – these aren't truths. The truth is, if the muscle is stressed enough to stimulate growth, it *will* grow – regardless of the rep range.

And oftentimes, your muscles are stressed the most on the first set, with diminishing returns as the sets continue and as the muscle fatigues. So, what does this mean? If you can stimulate growth in a few sets, you can finish your bodybuilding workout in a fraction of the time it currently takes you. Instead of 10x10 or whatever the set and rep scheme you use for your bodybuilding accessories, what if you took a couple of sets to failure and called it a day? I mean, if you applied the principle of specificity and actually stressed the muscle instead of just going through the motions, you will probably still make gains while also shaving down the amount of time you spend at the gym by a *lot*. In fact, a publication from December 2013 titled "Evidence-Based Resistance Training Recommendations for Muscular Hypertrophy," by Dr. James Fisher et al., supports this: The authors noted that, if you were to train a muscle group with multiple sets and exercises, taking just *one* set of each exercise to momentary muscle failure with utmost training intensity appeared to attain similar hypertrophy results as performing multiple sets of each exercise! [4]

But let's revisit Dr. Schoenfeld's meta-analysis, as it did reveal something important to take note of: When taking sets to failure, heavier loads at lower rep ranges resulted in a much greater 1RM increase than lighter loads at higher rep ranges. So, although you can build muscle at any rep range, research does support the existence of a strength-endurance continuum. The strength-endurance continuum exists because of the principle of specificity: You get better at what you do and how you train. The more strength training you do, the stronger you will be. The more endurance training you do, the better you will become at endurance activities. This explains why powerlifters perform heavy singles so often: Their sport literally consists of heavy singles.

So instead of being focused on the rep range you want to train at, decide on where you want to be on the strength-endurance continuum. If you favor strength, you will have to train with heavier loads, which will result in fewer reps when taking the sets to failure. If you favor endurance you will train using lighter loads and end up performing a lot more repetitions before reaching failure.

However, if your goal is primarily muscle growth, you should favor training with heavier loads because of the relationship between strength and size: Type II muscle fibers have higher potential for growth and are used more extensively when you are outputting large amounts of force. Thus, training with heavier loads allow you to recruit and train Type II muscle fibers more directly, resulting in faster and more potential for growth than if you were to train Type I muscle fibers with the same intensity.

Barbell Strength Training

Heavy lifting will result in faster gains, but do you *need* to partake in barbell strength training? No. There's nothing wrong with barbell strength training but, if your goal is primarily muscle growth, barbell strength training isn't necessary.

You see, *strength* adaptations are different from *muscular strength* adaptations. Increased muscular strength is due to an increase in contractile proteins, which will result in myofibrillar hypertrophy. Since hypertrophy is present, there will be increases in muscle size too. As such, there is a relationship between *muscular strength* and muscular size: An individual with more muscle mass would likely perform better than if they had less muscle mass provided everything else – like technical proficiency with the exercise, mental state, physical state, etc. – remains the same.

But *general* strength is different from muscular strength. It is possible for there to be *no* muscle adaptations when strength is increased. That's because strength is primarily a skill. *Strength is specific.* The more you perform a movement at maximal loads, the better you get at doing it. This is why powerlifters perform heavy squats so often – not only is it a lift in competition, but they need to practice squatting heavy weights to get good at it. Likewise, the more you perform the same movement but at lighter loads and higher repetitions, the better you will get at performing said movement at lighter loads and higher repetitions.

When you partake in barbell strength training or powerlifting training, you are training specifically for general strength – not muscular strength. Although muscular strength and myofibrillar hypertrophy can result as a byproduct of strength-specific training, it is secondary to becoming more proficient with the strength training exercises themselves. But since muscle size is also one of the factors for strength, strength athletes should consider performing bodybuilding isolation exercises in order to build muscle mass. [5] The opposite – bodybuilders taking up barbell strength training – is *not* mandatory, though I do recommend it for other reasons (which I will get to in Chapter 14).

Whether you – someone whose goals are primarily muscle growth – should partake in barbell strength training though is entirely up to you. There are a myriad number of benefits to strength training that you can find with a simple Google search. But there's another benefit: Some of the best exercises for building the chest and legs are also barbell strength training exercises too. And nothing's holding you back from treating multi-joint strength training exercises with an emphasis on internal cues like mind-muscle connection. You can even take your multi-joint strength training compound exercises to failure through AMRAP training (while doing your best to isolate the muscle group that you are trying to train) in order to fulfill the principles of specificity and overload.

However, if you would rather take a strength training approach to some exercises, avoid using AMRAP sets for them. The reason is because of the principle of specificity: Since motor learning and proficiency with the movement is a key player in how strong you are at a movement; it is better to perform higher quality repetitions than it is to perform low quality ones. Additionally, a meta-analysis published in April 2016 by Dr. Daniel Hackett et al. revealed that non-failure training with *compound* strength training exercises results in more strength than failure-training. [6] Although it was a small percentage improvement that is "unlikely to be meaningful," the risk of injuries involved with taking compound strength training exercises to failure is pretty high.

My recommendation would be non-failure strength training for compound exercises, where the primary focus is on getting better with the lift itself. However, bodybuilding isolation exercises should be taken to failure and executed with proper mind-muscle connection. Overall, big, strong muscle groups like the chest, quads and hamstrings will be built primarily using compound exercises, whereas other muscle groups will be built using mostly isolation exercises. Of course, you are free to train the compounds like you would isolations – by taking sets to failure and focusing exclusively on mind-muscle connection – if muscle growth is indeed your only goal. However, I think it is a good idea to have strength goals, and I will delve into why in Part II, Chapter 14.

Exercise Selection

Specificity matters a lot when it comes to exercise selection. If you want to train your muscles, the exercises you do should reflect that. This generally means using isolation movements, which makes it easier to keep the tension on your muscles. As opposed to training movements and getting bigger as a byproduct of getting stronger at said movements, isolation exercises train the muscles directly to force the muscle to grow.

And because you are training muscles, you will perform exercises that your muscles are meant to perform. This means curls for bicep growth, because elbow flexion is one of the primary functions of the biceps. Some muscles, like the pectorals and quadriceps, can handle a ton of stress. As such, the best way to train them is with compound exercises like the barbell bench press and the barbell back squat. Whether you approach compounds with a strength training approach or bodybuilding approach – where the emphasis is on loading the muscles – though is up to you. I go more in-depth about exercise selection in Part III.

Beginner lifters tend to vary the exercises they do often, thinking they need to "confuse" their muscles. But that's not true. In fact, exercises are *methods* you use to fulfill the principles of muscle growth. As such, whether you vary your exercises or not shouldn't matter if your goal is muscle growth. A study from 2019, conducted on 20 trained men with an average training age of 2.5 years, found that performing the same workout every session for 8 weeks resulted in similar growth when compared to a second group that cycled 4 different workouts. (The 4 different workouts varied in load, rest interval, number of sets performed and used slight variations of the same exercise.) [7] In other words, *your muscles don't need to be "confused."*

In fact, the term "muscle conclusion" is a marketing term with weak scientific backing. Like how muscle hyperplasia was used to sell inter-set stretching, "muscle confusion" was used to sell P90X – a home exercise regime. [8] Many direct response copywriters – the people who write infomercials – claim that all of P90X's earlier infomercials bombed, and that it wasn't until they came up with the "muscle confusion" gimmick that P90X took off.

That being said, while there are no definite "best" exercises, there may be certain exercises that are superior for you specifically. In other words, *why* and *how* you perform the exercises are what matters most. A 2017 study by Jacob Rauch et al. has shown that being able to choose exercises on the fly is actually superior for muscle growth when all other variables (training frequency, load, number of sets to failure) are equal. [9] Though there's no definite explanation for this yet, I speculate that – when given the choice – people will naturally gravitate towards exercises they are more familiar with. This familiarity means better execution of the movement and thus better mind-muscle connection. So, don't perform a behind-the-neck-snatch-grip overhead press just because it's written in your program when you've never done it before – your reason, your *why*, for doing the exercise is weak, and you likely don't even know *how* to perform it in a way that's best for hypertrophy. Sure, play around with it; learn it for the future. But never lose sight of the goal – which is building muscle, and not simply completing a workout program.

Tempo and Time under Tension

Like inter-set stretching, varying your training tempo (how fast you perform your reps) and how long your muscles are under tension (time under tension) are other training methods you can approach muscle growth with. But contrary to what many people may believe, performing reps slowly is *not* a principle of muscle growth.

In fact, Dr. Brad Schoenfeld et al. published a systematic review and meta-analysis in April 2015 revealing that reps performed between 0.5 seconds and 8 seconds produce very similar hypertrophic results. That means that performing reps relatively quickly (0.5 second) produces the same results as controlling the concentric and eccentric portions of a lift. Really slow repetitions, ones exceeding 10 seconds long, are actually inferior for muscle growth. [10] This dispels the common myth that slow reps lead to greater time under tension, which result in more muscle damage (via overload) and thus more growth.

However, that's not to say that you shouldn't control your repetitions. Performing controlled reps are important because they allow you to make sure you are using the correct muscles in a lift, which is crucial for the principle of specificity. I mean, if you're not training your muscles, why expect your muscles to grow? When your goal is muscular hypertrophy, you want to train muscles – not movements. As such, *slow* repetitions aren't mandatory, but controlled repetitions *are*. In fact, I'd argue that time under tension and tempo training should be used exclusively for the purposes of specificity, not overload – which is what most lifters use it for in this day and age. Don't slow your reps to make them harder; only slow them to ensure that you're training the correct muscles.

Now that you know the intricacies of rep ranges, the difference between training for muscular strength and training for general strength, and have a basic understanding of exercise selection and time under tension, let's cover the science behind the new formula for volume – which is the driving factor of muscle growth – in the next chapter. Read on.

Chapter 8:

The Science Behind Training Volume, Sets and Rest Intervals

When you start taking all your sets to failure, it can be easy to overdo it. As such, it is a good idea to determine upper and lower limits for training volume. If it is your first time taking all your sets to failure, consider using a training volume that is closer to the minimum effective dosages. You can always increase your volume as time goes on.

But first, the formula for volume has changed. Repetition volume, or volume as a product of sets and reps, is dated. Volume as a product of sets, reps, and load – sometimes referred to as tonnage or poundage – is also dated. If the most popular formulas for volume are invalid, how *do* you calculate volume?

Well, you must first understand what the concept of volume is. Volume originated because lifters, trainers and coaches wanted a way to quantify training. Without a way to quantify training, training couldn't be measured. And because what doesn't get measured cannot be improved, it becomes impossible to approach training scientifically.

Although both formulas of volume are widely accepted (both repetition volume and tonnage are still in use today), many top coaches have come up with their own different ways of quantifying training. Why? Because the previous formulas were flawed: You can accumulate a ton of volume through 10 sets of 10 hamstring curls, yet it wouldn't be as fatiguing as a couple near-max deadlift attempts.

World renowned coach and champion powerlifter Mike Tuchscherer took this into consideration and formulated training stress as the product of volume and psychological fatigue. Another renowned powerlifting coach and the only professor of powerlifting in the world, Boris Sheiko, considers training volume as 3 separate entities: total number of reps, poundage, and average intensity divided by the individual's 1RM. However, these are volume calculations for powerlifting, and building muscle is a *lot* simpler than powerlifting.

There are two principles of muscle growth that are in play during training – the principles of specificity and overload. So, for the purposes of muscle growth, volume has to somehow quantify training in a way that lets you measure specificity and overload on any given exercise and on any given rep. But if you apply mind-muscle connection to all your reps, you'd satisfy the principle of specificity. And if you take all those sets to muscle failure, you'd also satisfy the principle of overload. At that point, why not just count the number of AMRAP sets you perform for each muscle group?

For hypertrophy purposes, volume *is* as simple as counting the number of hard sets. [1] So if you were prescribed 4 sets of bicep curls but only 1 of the sets were hard, your training volume for biceps that session would be have been 1 set. On the other hand, if you took all 4 sets of curls to failure, you would have a training volume of 4 sets. It's really that simple: Counting the number of hard sets that you perform – which should be every set since you'll be taking them all to failure – makes it easy to quantify your training. In fact, most of the studies I've referenced so far measured volume this way, including the systematic reviews and meta-analyses.

It can be argued that maybe counting the number of hard sets only works for beginner lifters, who generally see gains doing any kind of resistance training. However, in July 2018, a systematic review published by Dr. Eneko Baz-Valle et al. supports the concept of simply counting the number of hard sets as volume, at least for hypertrophy purposes, for trained lifters too. The review, consisting of 14 studies featuring only trained lifters (lifters with at least 1 year of training experience), set out to determine whether volume can be simplified to the number of hard sets performed. And the results were clear: Counting the number of hard sets can accurately quantify volume and predict hypertrophy outcomes, even in trained lifters. [2]

There were some caveats according to Dr. Baz-Velle's review, though. For starters, the review noted that sets should ideally consist of 6+ repetitions. Although this isn't completely necessary – many people have put on a ton of muscle using sets of 5 whilst on 3x5 or 5x5 strength programs – using higher rep ranges does increases adherence to the principle of specificity. How? Higher rep ranges result in greater fatigue which in turn results in less efficient motor control. And as explained in Chapter 5, these inefficiencies in motor control result in the need for greater muscle activation to accomplish the same movement. In other words, higher rep ranges encourage the utilization of internal cues such as mind-muscle connection – primarily because, as you fatigue, your attention slowly shifts from external cues such as simply performing the movement to internal cues such as fighting fatigue and forcing your muscles to work.

Additionally, Dr. Baz-Velle's review found it unnecessary to reach complete failure with each set, suggesting that stopping sets with 3 or fewer repetitions from failure is enough. However, this must be contrasted with the study discussed in Chapter 1: When 160 trained lifters performed a rep-max with the load they generally used for 10 reps on the bench press, only 22% of them were self-selecting loads that were 3 or fewer repetitions from failure. In other words, only 22% of lifters were selecting loads that allowed them to train hard enough to stimulate muscle growth! And these were trained lifters who are supposed to be much better at self-selecting loads for training than beginner lifters! As such, taking sets to failure is a more surefire way of adhering to the principle of overload.

There are other flaws with counting the number of hard sets as volume too, though. For example, what if you were looking to train the chest with the incline press? 4 sets of incline presses would result in a volume of 4 sets for the chest; but would it also count towards volume for the anterior deltoids (the front of the shoulders), which are used a lot in the incline press? When it comes down to it, supporting muscle groups don't do as much work as the main movers, or muscle groups whose primary function is the exercise itself, so the short answer is no. I will go in greater detail regarding muscle groups, their functions and how it affects volume in Part III.

Although how you measure volume has changed, volume being the driving factor behind muscle growth remains to be true. A systematic review and meta-analysis published by Dr. Brad Schoenfeld et al. in

June 2017, reveals that each additional set you perform increases your effect size by up to 0.37%. Thus, the number of sets is directly correlated to how much gains you make. The study also revealed that doing at least 10 sets per week per muscle group seems to result in greater gains than doing less than 10 sets. [3] As such, a lower limit of 10 sets per week per muscle group is a good starting point. If you are training with the minimum frequency of twice a week, this would result in 5 sets per training session.

Is there an upper limit on how much volume you can handle per week? Multiple studies – some with volumes up to 45 sets per week for a muscle group – have shown that muscle size increases as weekly volume increases, though strength tends to decrease at higher weekly volumes. [4][5] Another study also supports the idea that more volume leads to greater increases in muscle size, but claims that the increases in muscle size from very high levels of volume are mostly due to swelling or exercise-induced inflammation. [6] Despite none of these studies being either systematic reviews or meta-analyses, the trend seems to point towards diminishing returns when it comes to pushing very high levels of volume. So, theoretically, there is no limit: The more volume you perform the bigger your muscles. But the consequences – reduced strength and the fact that most of your size gains are from swelling and inflammation – outweigh the diminishing returns that you would make with very high levels of training volume. Thus, start with 10 sets per muscle group per week for now, and worry about higher training volumes only when you've hit a plateau.

What about volume per training session? I mean if you were prescribed 15 sets for a muscle group, you can't possibly make optimal gains by performing all 15 sets in the same training session, right? Well, it seems that there *is* a limit as to how much volume you can accumulate in a training session, and that's where volume's relationship with frequency comes in.

In short, limit yourself to a training volume of 4 to 6 AMRAP sets per muscle group per day. Why? A study published in November 2017 by Dr. Daniel Hackett et al. revealed that a control group performing 5x10 (5 sets of 10) walked away with *significantly* greater increases in lean body mass and strength than another group performing 10x10 (10 sets of 10) of the same program. This suggests that too much volume on any given day can be detrimental to your gains. The study concluded that, to maximize hypertrophic training effects, it is recommended to accumulate no more than 4-6 AMRAP sets of volume per muscle group per training session. [7] Although not a systematic review or meta-analysis, accumulating 4-6 sets per training session agrees with the baseline weekly volume of 10 sets and the baseline training frequency of twice weekly found by 2 other meta-analyses.

Now let's consider the hypothetical scenario that you were to train a muscle group 5 times a week with 2 hard sets per session. This hypothetical scenario is near ideal: You have a training frequency greater than once a week, a total weekly volume of at least 10 sets per week, and you are within the upper limit of 4 to 6 AMRAP sets per session. But are 2 sets per training session really enough to stimulate muscle growth? Contrary to the common belief that you need to annihilate a muscle group each training session, a study published September 2018 by professor Cauê Vazquez La Scala Teixeria found that performing just 2 hard sets per training session was indeed enough to maximize muscle growth. So long as weekly training volume consists of 10+ sets and that each set was challenging, performing <3 sets per session results in similar muscle growth to performing ≥3 sets per session – in both untrained and trained individuals. [8] Thus, you can maximize bicep growth by simply showing up to the gym every day for less than 10 minutes a session by simply taking 2 sets of bicep curls to failure! If you think this is too good to be true, just remember that Dr. James Fisher et al. wrote an evidence-based publication in 2013 that stated taking just *one* set of each exercise to muscle failure can indeed result in the same gains as training with multiple sets of the same exercises. [9]

When Should You Increase Training Volume?

Increasing training volume should be the last thing you do to address a training plateau. In other words, increasing your training volume is only a consideration when a plateau has *truly* occurred and not because of other reasons. If you're not obeying the principle of specificity and cheating far too much on your reps to engage the proper muscle groups – fix it.

If you're not obeying the principle of consistency and have adherence problems – fix it. If you're not training hard enough – as in you're not obeying the principle of overload – fix it. If your diet is off... if you're struggling to get quality sleep... if there's too much stress in life... whatever the problem – FIX IT. Once all these fixes have been implemented and the only stone left unturned is an increase in volume, then – and only then – should you increase your training volume.

Simply encountering a plateau does not mean you should increase your training volume and train more. Even though volume may be the primary driver of muscle growth, *volume itself is still not a principle of muscle growth.* If your execution of a rep is subpar, meaning you're failing to adhere to the principle of specificity, what makes you think doing more subpar reps is the right way to go about it? It's about quality – not quantity. And by limiting yourself to lower levels of volume, such as 10 sets per muscle group per week, you force yourself to make every rep productive. There's no room for bad reps that don't adhere to the principle of specificity. Likewise, it makes no sense to train *more* if you're not adhering to the principle of overload. It is entirely possible to do 10 sets of 10 for every muscle group, spending hours at the gym, and still make fewer gains than someone taking 2 sets to failure in under 10 minutes. Think quality, not quantity.

Rest Intervals

This then begs the question: How long should you rest between sets? Surprisingly, rest intervals don't impact muscle growth much. Although rest intervals *can* have an impact on how many reps you perform on each set, and thus total rep count per training session, the results are insignificant when volume – calculated by counting the number of AMRAP sets or sets taken to failure – is equated. [9] This means doing 5 AMRAP sets with 30 seconds rest will result in very similar muscle growth as doing 5 AMRAP sets with 90 seconds rest, provided that you take all sets to failure.

Sure, training with longer rests will result in a higher total repetition count, but repetition count is not necessarily an indicator of muscle growth. How much stress the muscle goes through is a better indicator of muscle growth. This is why volume as a product of sets and reps was retired in the first place, and why counting the number of hard sets has replaced it.

Drop Sets, Supersets, Giant Sets, etc.

Like inter-set stretching, drop sets, supersets and giant sets are all methods of training that encourage you to train harder in order to fulfill the principle of overload. As such, they all have a place in training – specifically drop sets, which are great for individuals who fail to adhere to the principle of overload. For everyone else, implementing training methods like drop sets, supersets and giant sets allow you to finish your workouts faster. Note that they are methods – regardless if you use them or not, most of your gains will come from you adhering to the principles. Thus, think of these techniques as merely tools to manage time spent at the gym and to quicken your workouts.

However, although principles are important, they don't work alone: Principles *need* methods. While principles are fundamental truths or laws, methods are tangible and systematic. Without methods, principles are just that – abstract ideas. Principles depend on methods to give them form. So, while principles still dictate whether you build muscle or not, it is the methods that decide everything else – such as how long your workouts are and whether you adhere to your training program in the first place. If you'd like a leg up against everyone else by employing some of the best methods for muscle growth, go to www.andyxiong.com/bonus/hypertrophy for some bonuses – including a list of methods I personally use and how to implement them.

Chapter 9:

The Science and History of Intensity and Load

Depending on whom you ask intensity and load can mean the same thing or something completely different. If you've ever dabbled from bodybuilding training to powerlifting training, or vice versa, you would know what I mean: In the world of bodybuilding intensity was once a measure of how hard you train, but in the world of strength training it is a percentage of your 1RM. What gives?

To define intensity, let's first define load. Load is the weight you use when doing a specific exercise. It is usually a percentage of your rep maxes, with most training programs using a percentage of your 1RM. In other words, intensity in the world of strength training, powerlifting and Olympic weightlifting refers to load. For example, an intensity of 70% refers to a load that is 70% of your 1RM in barbell strength training and powerlifting programs. But in the scientific world, these percentages are referred to as "percentage load."

So how did the word intensity end up in the position where it describes load? In the bodybuilding world, intensity is a measure of the effort of training. Training with high intensity means training with the intent to overload the muscle. Low intensity training, like low intensity cardio, means low impact training. You can kind of already see how the definition of intensity shifted in the world of strength training: It is easier to prescribe the load, rep and set scheme in a quantifiable way than it is to describe how much effort you should put into training. For example, as a coach, you can tell your athlete to perform 5 reps of squats at a high intensity because you think that the training adaptations that come with it is what your athlete needs, but to the athlete it is vague and ambiguous. So why not just prescribe the exact load, exact set and exact rep scheme to get as close to the training response that you wanted to prescribe in the first place?

In other words, which would you prefer I tell you: Perform a set of 5 squats at a very high intensity, or perform a set of 5 squats at 85%? The latter is clearer and much less ambiguous.

But when you're taking all your sets to failure, the loads you train at shouldn't matter. A 17-week study published in October 2018 by Bruce M. Lima et al. found that, while taking all sets to failure, reducing load by 10% per set led to a lower perception of effort than using the same load for all sets. Yet, reducing load by 10% per set resulted in similar hypertrophy (and strength) adaptations as using the same load for all sets. In other words, performing sets to failure at 80%, 72% and 64.8%, for example, resulted in the same gains as performing 3 sets to failure at 80%. [1] This study suggests that training intensity, and thus adherence to the principle of overload, matters much more than training load. In other words, the golden hypertrophy range of 8-12 or 6-15 reps is not so golden anymore – especially if you aren't taking those sets to failure.

However, current evidence advises against training with a load less than 30% unless you are using special training methods like occlusion or blood-flow restriction. This is because training at such low percentages requires performing an extraordinarily high number of reps in order to stimulate growth. Type II muscle fibers, the ones that grow more quickly and can produce more force, are easily fatigued. This means that high rep, low load sets generally stimulate Type I muscle fiber growth. Type I muscle fibers are more responsible for endurance and has a much smaller impact on muscle size. Unless you are an endurance athlete, most of your training will happen in the medium to high load range to elicit hypertrophy and strength gains, as utmost training effort here recruits as many motor units and muscle fibers as possible. [2]

Now if you've dabbled in the powerlifting scene, you have probably already noticed a shift back towards "intensity" as we know it in the bodybuilding world. More and more training programs are employing the use of RPE, or rate of perceived exertion, which is literally *a scale from 0-10 describing the intensity of a set or workout*. Was the set moderate intensity? RPE 5. Intense but not too challenging? RPE 8. Requiring the highest intensity of effort to complete?

RPE 10. Why is this happening? Because, like how repetition volume is a bad indicator of training stress, *intensity as a percentage or load is also a bad indicator of training stress*. For example, individuals who have been squatting heavy sets of 5's for a while now will find sets of 5 squats at 85% tolerable, whereas people who have never touched high percentages or who have never touched anything more than doubles (sets of 2's) would find it absolutely brutal. And because what we're all after is the right amounts of training stress for the right training adaptations, strength athletes who use RPE adjust the load accordingly until they get the desired RPE – or in other words, intensity.

Thus, the concept of RPE isn't new; its literally what intensity used to be, but in a more quantifiable way. And bodybuilders, in a way, have been using something like RPE for decades already. Regardless, powerlifting champion Mike Tuchscherer, founder and head coach of Reactive Training Systems (RTS), deserves praise for popularizing the use of RPE and shifting the focus from numbers-based training, where you blindly follow a program "optimized" to give you the right training stress, to more of a principles-based training system where training comes first and programming comes second. And, as you will soon see in the next chapter, this is true for another variable of programming... Read on.

Chapter 10:

The Science Behind Periodization and How to Avoid Overtraining

Believe it or not, periodization isn't important when your goal is primarily muscle growth. That's not to say that periodization is a scam though: Periodization is of utmost important when you are training for performance. To understand why periodization isn't important for muscle growth though, you must understand why periodization is so popular in the first place.

Periodization is a means to predict and direct training patterns. An athlete may need to perform his or her best at a competition, and periodization allows the coach to program in a way that the athlete is in peak condition when needed. For example, powerlifters and Olympic weightlifters periodize their training to ensure that their performance on the platform is their absolute best, as do strongman competitors. Sports athletes have also been using different methods of periodization since the 1950s; the way athletes train in the offseason is different from the way they train in preseason and peak season.

In other words, periodization is a scientific way of approaching training by manipulating training variables to produce different adaptations at different times. It can be as simple as going from high volume, low load training to low volume, high load training over the period of weeks or months. Of course, other periodization methods, like undulating periodization, exist too.

However, building muscle, at its simplest, is about progressively overloading the muscle. If you do that, *how* you periodize your program should not matter. A systematic review and meta-analysis from June 2017, published by Dr. Brad Schoenfeld et al., has shown that periodized and non-periodized training routines result in very similar muscle gains. [1] Subsequently, a systematic review and meta-analysis performed in August 2017 by Dr. Jojo Grgic et al. revealed that when training *is* periodized, different methods of periodization seem to also result in similar muscle growth. [2]

Whether you periodize your training or not doesn't seem to affect muscular hypertrophy. But I can think of some individuals who could benefit from periodization: People who dislike routine, people who hate training the same way every day, people who get upset when progression isn't linear, and people who hate plateaus should consider running a periodized training program. Why? Because periodization can improve adherence to a program by removing the negative feelings associated with encountering plateaus. Consistency is a *key* principle of muscle growth after all.

Otherwise, if you have no problems adhering to a program, you can easily avoid overtraining by keeping your weekly volumes on the lower end and only increasing it ever so slightly. As explained in Chapter 8, increasing volume in order to break plateaus is sometimes the *wrong* solution. In fact, a training volume of 10 sets per muscle group per week can probably build you muscle *for years*; primarily because your mind-muscle connection will continue to sharpen, leading to higher quality repetitions and better specificity when it comes to building muscle. Heck, increasing volume only makes sense if you have all the other principles nailed down first.

Again, note that this is for muscular hypertrophy, not strength training. If you are a strength athlete (powerlifter, Olympic weightlifter, or strongman competitor), periodization is likely mandatory for you to excel at your sport. But for people who care only about building muscle, periodization is completely and utterly unnecessary.

Part II

The Principle of Consistency, Motivation, Goal Setting and Plateaus

ANDY XIONG

Chapter 11:

The Importance of Being Motivated Beyond Yourself

Large pectoral muscles, washboard abs, arms that fill out the sleeves; these are some of the things that guys generally want. Others may want broad shoulders, a thick back, swole traps, or maybe just slightly bigger calves. It is important to have a vision of what you want and where you want to be, but it is even more important to know *why*. This is fundamentally the most important, and most overlooked, factor for success at anything in life.

Going to the gym for the first time is perhaps one of the greatest victories in your fitness journey, primarily because there is a lot of inertia when it comes to doing something new. But going once isn't going to give you the results that you want. Going only once doesn't fulfill a key principle of muscle growth – consistency. Although you may have found the motivation you needed to start going to the gym, oftentimes you need *much* stronger motivators in order to hit the gym consistently. And if your goal is to achieve some *big* dreams, you are going to require some very strong motivators.

Before enrolling in university, I was a casual calisthenics practitioner following a Navy Seals workout I found off Bodybulding.com. Although I didn't train often, I was serious when I *did* train – which was only 2 months a year. I would get up at 5:00 a.m., jog at 6:00 a.m. for at least 2-miles, and end my workout at the playground near my home around 7:30 a.m. Then I'd go home, wash up and spend the rest of the day playing video games. I was dedicated, but I wasn't dedicated enough to train throughout the year; it was something I did only during the summer. And even though I was dedicated, I wasn't dedicated enough to fix my other bad habits. I wouldn't even change my diet. I lacked a strong reason to. I lacked a strong *why*.

I had always wanted bigger arms, a large chest and shredded abs. I wanted a body like those found on Bodybuilding.com. But even when I enrolled in university and had access to, perhaps, one of the best gyms in the downtown core, I still wouldn't set foot in the gym unless friends were going. Why? I was *afraid* and lacked confidence. If marketing has taught me one thing, it was that fear was one of the best motivators for action. But that meant that it was a strong motivator for inaction, too. Though my motivators changed as time went on, the feeling of fear continued to overpower my *why*, which was to become a better version of myself.

Then one day, my friend Philly explained how he brought his back squat from a meager 185 lbs. for 5 reps to a single at 405 lbs. in about a year of strength training. I was blown away. Philly was squatting more than my peers who had been training for several years! This motivated me so much that I conquered my fear of going to the gym alone, and I started grinding right away. Suddenly, I was a lot more consistent with hitting the gym, and progress sped up.

In 14 months, I brought my squat to 405 lbs., upped it to 425 lbs. in another 3 weeks, and again to 440 lbs. 3 months later, all at a bodyweight of no more than 174 lbs. My metabolism was fast, I was healthy and –

although I was skipping all my classes and spending almost 4 hours at the gym per session – life was good. And I attribute all of this to my new *why*: I wanted to inspire others like Philly once did to me. *I wanted to motivate and inspire others to better themselves.*

When you are motivated beyond yourself you can accomplish great things. But if you want to continue achieving great things, you should never forget what motivated you in the first place. And unfortunately, my goals changed. I no longer wanted to motivate and inspire others. Although I may have told others that it was one of the reasons I trained, stepping foot in the gym was ultimately something that I did for myself. It was a source of pleasure. I'd always have at least 1 or 2 close friends to train with, and sometimes up to 10 close buddies, and we'd be the loud obnoxious gym bros at our gym. Lifting became something I used to feed my ego and confidence... and that's when the gains stopped coming.

Why you do something is super important. Once my motivation for lifting switched from motivating and inspiring others to one of pleasure, my life slowly crumbled. I continued to skip all my classes, went to bed between 4 a.m. and 6 a.m., woke up around 1:00 p.m., and stayed in bed until 3:00 p.m. every day. Why? Because I had no reason to get up early. My source of pleasure, my life purpose, was to train. And because my gym closed at 11 p.m., all I had to do was get into the gym before 8:00 p.m. at the latest.

For many, money is a great motivator. Many of us are willing to work jobs that we hate in order to make some money. But money as a motivator didn't work for me and, unless you are trying to monetize your gains, it's probably not the greatest motivator to start training in the first place. In fact, for me, pleasure was a bigger motivator than money ever was and probably ever will be. When I had a job, I would regularly show up 2 to 3 hours late because I wanted to squeeze a workout in before going to work. Training, in my opinion, was more important than money. And when I decided to take the self-employment route, I made the most money I'd ever made in my 4th month of freelancing and entrepreneurship – only to get bored, lose motivation and have my cash flow slip ever since.

Today, I realize that you must have a purpose that is bigger than yourself; that all your actions should align with said purpose; and that you should never forget said purpose. The most successful businesses do this – in the form of a mission statement. And if a one-sentence mission statement is enough to inspire and motivate thousands of employees to move in one right direction and in unison, what do you think the right motivator can do for *you*?

Pleasure is fun and all, but it won't give you a reason to get out of bed. For me, money was an even worse motivator than pleasure was – but I may be in the minority here. (Though I'm pretty sure once most of you hit your income goals, you too will lose the motivation to work for money.) For me, helping others is what encourages me to go to bed early, get up early, say "no" to partying and drinking, and maintain a regular routine these days. I love helping people accomplish their goals – I love it so much that it's my purpose now. Their success is my success. Their happiness is my happiness. So, my question to you is: Why do *you* want to build more muscle?

You probably want to be more confident, but what for? What's your motive? What's your goal? What's your purpose? And how does building muscle fit into all this? Of course, you don't have to know yet: You can still make a ton of progress being driven by pleasure or money. But if building muscle aligns with your purpose in life, you will find it that much easier to make gains.

Knowing your why is only the first step though. In the next chapter, I cover the importance of proper goal setting. Your *why* will give you purpose, but your vision and goals are what gives you direction. Read on.

Chapter 12:

The Importance of Setting Proper Goals and Having a Plan

Whatever you want to achieve in your fitness journey, it all starts with a motive – your *why* – and a goal. And if you have a motive, you have already taken the first step – so why not complete the walk?

Without a goal you are directionless. You have nowhere to go. You have nothing to strive for; you are purposeless. You will achieve nothing because there is nothing that you want to achieve. Only after you've decided on your goals will you know what steps you must take in order to achieve them.

But not everyone has goals. I see it all the time. People come to the gym, perform some curls, do some cardio, and then call it a day. They come to the weight room for the sake of coming, but they do not make progress and achieve nothing. After a while, a lot of people give up due to their lack of progress and decide not to show up anymore. This is because they had nothing to strive for. When you have nothing to strive for, no amount of motivation or willpower will help you accomplish anything. Throw in the fact that you won't see results doing this and you can imagine why so many people give up.

I was guilty of not having goals either, primarily because I saw the gym as a source of pleasure. After obtaining a 440 lb. squat, I would come to the gym 3 to 4 times a week for over a year and a half to add a measly 10 lbs. to my back squat. I was consistent with my training and I trained hard; but because I had no clear vision of my goals, I had nothing to push for. Sure, I wanted a bigger squat – having been stuck at 440 lbs. for over a year at the time was infuriating – but it wasn't something I actively pushed for. I knew I wanted my back squat to go up, but I did not have a goal of where I wanted my squat to be. Had I had proper goals for my back squat, I could have added way more than 10 lbs. over a year and a half of training. And although I did have a goal of squatting over 500 lbs. for reps when I first started training, I did not have a *SMART goal*.

Your goals need to be SMART, meaning they must be **s**pecific, **m**easurable, **a**chievable, **r**elevant to where you currently are in life, and **t**ime bound. Consider the following two goals:

1. I want to lose weight
2. I want to lose 10 lbs. in 10 weeks so that I can fit in these pants and feel good about myself again

The first goal is an example of how you shouldn't set your goals. It's ambiguous, especially when compared to the second, SMART goal. Read the two goals out loud and you would realize that the second goal is a lot more empowering. Unlike goal #1, SMART goals aren't something you throw out meaninglessly in casual conversations.

And that was my mistake. My goal was ambiguous; it was not SMART. And I paid for it, throwing away over a year of training, by not knowing what I had to do to achieve my "goal" because I didn't really have a goal. Don't make the same mistake as me. If you don't clearly define what your goals are, you might as well not have any goals to begin with.

Have a Goal but Be Process Driven

While having a goal is important, it's not enough to succeed. In his bestselling book, *Atomic Habits*, James Clear noted that winners and losers often have the same goals. Yet, losers are still losers. For example, everyone who competes in Mr. Olympia has the goal of winning, but realistically there could only be *one* winner. Clear noted that while multiple people can have the same goals, it is the processes (or, as he calls it, systems) that differ.

As such, don't be results-oriented. Being results-oriented will only restrict your happiness. In the previous example, simply competing for Mr. Olympia meant you had one of the best physiques around; just because you didn't win the title of Mr. Olympia doesn't mean that you aren't already successful in your own right. And while all Mr. Olympia competitors may share a similar goal, it is their processes that brought them there in the first place. It is their processes that separated them from the 99%.

Thus, instead of being results-oriented, be process driven. Being process driven means focusing on your processes in relation to, and instead of, your goals. Do your processes align with your goals? If your goal is to lose weight, are you sticking to your diet on a daily basis? If your goal is to put on muscle mass, are you adhering to the principles of muscle growth? Even if you don't achieve your specific goal, having the right processes in place will ensure that you were at least headed in the right direction.

When you think in terms of processes, you might realize that your goals need to be changed and/or redefined. That's because being process driven often requires you to work backwards from your biggest goals in order to determine what steps you must make daily and what sub goals you must accomplish and by when. As an example, consider my post-secondary education. My goal was to graduate from university and earn a bachelor's in computer science on time (meaning in no more than 4 years) and without failing any of the 40 required courses. While it's a SMART goal, the results weren't as I had hoped: While I did accomplish my goal, I didn't actually learn anything – not because I went in knowing a lot and learned nothing of value, but I legitimately went in knowing *nothing* and graduated knowing *nothing*. My processes, which were determined from my faulty goal, didn't require me to learn anything: So long as I did the bare minimum to pass, I would have accomplished my goal. And that's exactly what had happened. Despite it being a SMART goal, it wasn't necessarily a good goal because it did not change my core identity.

In other words, simply setting SMART goals won't change who you are. You will remain the same person until you start taking consistent action. However, being process driven changes who you are, simply by changing your habits. When you avoid junk food because your goal is to be healthy, you're no longer someone with the goal of being healthy – you *are* a healthier person.

Being process driven means changing your identity, and a new identity is what results in long-term change. And the simplest process you can adhere to today is to find a workout program and follow it.

The Importance of Following a Workout Program

One way to ensure that you make progress towards achieving your goals is to follow a detailed workout program tailored for what you want to achieve. It can be one that you have written yourself, a program you have purchased, or a program you found online for free. It can even be the program I provide you for free at the back of this book. The details don't matter as long as it is a program that will move you in the right direction: towards your goals.

You will find that when you improvise your workouts you tend to a waste a lot of time and get a lot less done. On the other hand, when you already know what you must do because you are following a program, you are much more likely to focus on execution. But without a plan, you'd only waste time and energy thinking about what you *should* be doing. If you fail to plan, you to plan to fail: The more hesitation there is, the more room there is for error; and the less likely you are to achieve your goals. You must move towards your goals with confidence, otherwise you will subconsciously believe that you *can't* achieve said goals. And you cannot move towards your goals with confidence unless you know what you need to do or where you need to be. Hence why daily routines are so effective at producing productivity: They remove decision fatigue and distractions and focus exclusively on your habits and discipline.

For now, imagine your goal as the destination and your workout program as the map. A good program will put you on a path that leads you to your destination. Of course, you can wander around without a map and still manage to stumble onto your destination, but the fastest and most direct path will always include a map. If you were lost in a forest and it was a matter of life or death you would want a map, wouldn't you?

Having a goal and knowing the destination is the first step, but without a road map your goal is nothing but a dream. You need to follow a plan and have the right processes in order to tackle your goals. So, whereas a motive – or *why* – gives you purpose, a goal provides you with a tangible vision of where you want to be; a plan would be your map towards the vision; and your processes will determine whether you succeed or not.

Chapter 13:

Self-Management Secrets for Success

While we talked about motivators earlier and why it is fundamentally important, there is another powerful tool you can use to ensure adherence to the principle of consistency. But first, let's talk about motivation because motivation is where everything starts. However, people tend to think that that's where it ends too – but that's just wrong.

When you are motivated to do something, you will feel an incredible drive to start. However, motivation comes and goes. You can be motivated at one moment and unmotivated the next. It is like an emotion – but we don't have that much control over our emotions. As such, motivation is an unreliable source to proactively starting something new. Besides, you may be motivated to start an activity but then have that motivation slowly fade away as you proceed to execute said activity. Motivation is not a long-term solution to getting things done, and you will fail to hit your goals if you depend solely on motivation.

When you lack motivation, you can sometimes brute force yourself to doing things with willpower. However, like motivation, willpower has its flaws. Willpower is limited; it has a reserve. You would think that the more you exercise willpower, the more you will have of it. But this is false. Every time you force yourself to do something because of willpower, you will find it increasingly difficult to call upon it later in the day. If you have ever worked a job that you hated, you would be able to relate: After exercising willpower to get through the workday, you return home unwilling to do anything except unwind in front of the TV. Yet, this time could be used to develop a side hustle so that you can eventually quit the job that you hate. But because you ran out of willpower, you will find it excruciatingly hard to do anything but recharge.

On the other hand, building good habits is a much better solution than either motivation or willpower. While motivation can come and go, habits stay with you for a very long time. And whereas willpower can be expended, the more you exercise your habits the stronger they become. Habits are powerful but they can be good *or* bad. You can make training a habit, but you can also make skipping training sessions a habit too. Smoking and sleeping late are also examples of bad habits. And although you can break bad habits, it is extremely challenging to do so. In fact, breaking bad habits often mean replacing them with good ones instead.

A step further than habits is integration. If you are serious about training or healthy living, integrate it into your life or make your life *all* about training or healthy living. Finding the time to train can be a nightmare sometimes, but if training is your priority you will *make* the time to train. It is a matter of priorities, coupled with good habits – not motivation or willpower.

Lastly, there is something very powerful that you can do to help you achieve your goals: Change your environment. "Show me your friends and I'll show you your future." "You become like the 5 people you spend the most time with." You probably hear those sayings a lot, but do you take it to heart? If your goal is to be a high-level bodybuilding competitor, why would you continue to train at a commercial gym? You want to be surrounded by like-minded individuals who can understand your struggles, not people who tell you that your goals are fantasy – or worse, people who judge you. You are a product of your environment. Both you and your environment influence each other; you can't have one without the other. Thus, if you are willing to invest in changing yourself, make sure to invest in changing your environment too.

Changing your environment doesn't necessarily mean making big changes like finding a new gym or moving across the country to train at one of the best gyms available. You can always start small. Something as simple as leaving your smartphone in a locker can result in you being a lot more productive with your gym time. When you are not bombarded by the endless universe that is the Internet, you will be a lot more focused on your task at hand. That means a stronger mind-muscle connection and shorter training sessions.

Enforcing good habits, integrating training into your lifestyle, and changing your environment can have a profound impact on you achieving your goals – either by helping you realize your true potential, or by removing unnecessary noise so that you focus only on your goals. Now think: How can you apply this to your life right now? What bad habits do you need to get rid of? What good habits should you consider building? What changes can you make to your environment?

Chapter 14:

How to Tackle Plateaus and Stay Motivated

As stated earlier, encountering plateaus can be very demotivating. Human beings love the feeling of progress, but plateaus can remove all feelings of progress and leave us unmotivated. And when you are unmotivated, it can be difficult for you to set foot in the gym again. This in turn makes it that much more challenging for you to adhere to the principle of consistency and, subsequently, the principle of progressive overload. In this chapter, we cover how to tackle and avoid plateaus in order to prevent the feeling that no progress is being made.

Plateaus Differ from Unrealistic Expectations and Unsatisfactory Results

Oftentimes, you *are* making progress, but you just don't feel like you are. Maybe you're comparing your month-to-month progress to someone else's and feel as if you aren't where you should be. Other times, you probably have unrealistically high expectations in the back of your mind.

You must keep in mind that muscle gains, like fat loss, will differ from one person to another. Individuals who are on the leaner side will give off the impression that they are making faster progress because their muscles are much more visible, whereas individuals on the fluffier side may not even notice their muscle gains because of the excess layer of fat. That's why I encourage individuals who are new to training to cut down and lose weight when they start lifting: It can be really motivating to be able to see progress at the beginning of your lifting career. But if you're in a caloric surplus, look beyond the scale to make sure that you are gaining muscle and not fat. You should rely on the things you see in the mirror, and perhaps even make use of a measuring tape to measure your progress.

Similarly, it is also important to keep track of your training. Keeping a training log can be as important as following the correct training program. Although you don't have to keep track of the loads you use or your reps when using a principles-based training methodology (because loads and rep counts don't matter when you're taking sets to failure), tracking them down can help you pinpoint strength gains. If you ever need to adjust your volume levels, perhaps because of an injury or because you aren't progressing, having a journal to reflect on can aid you in future programming.

It is also important to note that your muscle gains won't be uniform, so don't expect yourself to gain a certain amount of muscle mass per week. There is no reason to be impatient when building muscle. At the beginning, it may take a while before you start seeing progress – sometimes up to 6 consecutive months. However, once you do notice the progress you've made, you'd realize how big of a change it really is. But don't expect to progress at this rate all the time.

"Beginner gains" is a term for the immense progress that is possible at the start of resistance training. However, many individuals get addicted to this rate of progression and expect it to happen despite entering the intermediate stages of their training career, which is a big mistake because gains aren't linear.

Lastly, you can't expect to look like a fitness model immediately. Oftentimes, they have perfect lighting, practiced posing extensively, or used filters or Photoshop to enhance their look. As such, you shouldn't be comparing yourself to anyone else but yourself: The most important part of training and personal development is being better than the person you were yesterday.

Tackling Plateaus caused by A Lack of Specificity

I once thought that if I combined strength training compounds with bodybuilding isolation accessories, I could reap the best of both worlds. But because I did all my pressing, squatting and deadlifting compounds with the intent of getting better at the lifts, I probably could have made a lot more progress in terms of muscle growth for my chest, quads, and hamstrings if I had decided to adhere to the principle of specificity and trained them using mind-muscle connection instead.

When it comes to muscle growth, adhering to the principle of specificity means actually using and training your muscles. In other words, you must use your *muscles* to perform the movements. Not momentum; not stretch reflexes or bounces; not ideal moment arms; but your muscles. This differs from barbell strength training and especially powerlifting, where you attempt to maximize your leverages in order to make lifting more weight easier. (As an extreme example of maximizing your leverages in order to lift more weight, Google "exorcist bench press.")

You must understand how to keep tension on the muscle, as well as what range of motion will work best for each exercise you perform. Sometimes, full range of motion can take tension off the muscle, but you won't know this unless you really have your mind-muscle connection nailed down. In fact, partial reps have been shown to allow for greater hypertrophy in exercises where it's difficult to keep tension on the target muscle throughout its full range of motion: A 2019 study performed with trained men found that barbell triceps extensions done with a partial range of motion can produced nearly twice as much hypertrophy. [1] As such, when training with muscle growth in mind, you may be required to use lighter loads than if you were using a strength training approach to ensure proper mind-muscle connection.

Likewise, cardiovascular and conditioning workouts should not make up the bulk of your program if your goal is to increase muscle size. If you can recover completely between workouts feel free to add some cardio sessions in every now and then, but you should not overdo it, or it may hurt your recovery. If you want to perform cardiovascular work, look into a combination of high-intensity interval training (HIIT) and very low intensity cardiovascular work like walking or hiking.

Tackling Plateaus caused by Lack of Overload

Often, plateaus are the result of a lack of overload. Aside from not training hard enough, the only other way to not adhere to the principle of overload is if you aren't performing enough volume. Not because you don't want to though, but usually because of a lack of time.

If you find yourself unable to train hard enough to stimulate muscle growth, you can opt to include drop sets into your training. Drop sets make use of sub-maximal loads that are performed right after a set was taken to failure for several more sets to ensure overload. For example, after taking a set of dumbbell bicep curls to failure, immediately grab another pair of lighter dumbbells and continue to perform reps until you hit failure again. You can even perform another drop set right after that, though I would only count the initial AMRAP set towards the volume count (meaning don't count drop sets towards total training). Regardless, drop sets help ensure overload.

While I could get into time management and self-management tips for those of you who fail to adhere to the principle of overload due to a lack of training time, I think utilizing different training methods are much more applicable. In fact, what you could do is substitute out isolation exercises in exchange for fewer compound movements. For example, instead of performing 10 AMRAP sets for both the chest and the anterior deltoids per week, you can opt for 10 AMRAP bench sets instead. Both the pectorals and the anterior deltoids are used extensively in the bench press, meaning you can drop direct anterior deltoid training. You can even use the bench press to build the triceps too, effectively cutting down the total number of sets from a sum of 30 sets a week for 3 different muscle groups to 10 sets of bench presses a week. Other compounds – like squats, bent-over rows, military presses, deadlifts, dips and pull-ups – can work too. Compound exercises train some of the largest muscles in your body, and the larger these get the bigger your frame and the bigger you will look with clothes on. While it's not an ideal way to train if your goal is to maximize muscle growth, it's better than skipping workouts entirely because you don't think you have enough time to train.

Training methods like supersets and giant sets are also great tools to use if time is of the essence. Perform a chest exercise like the bench press and superset it with a back exercise, like the bent-over row, to trim down the total time you spend resting in the gym. Resting tends to take up most of the time people spend at the gym, so supersets are a great option to ensure that your time at the gym is time spent productively. Giant sets are the same as supersets but consist of even more exercises. For more information on training methods, go to www.andyxiong.com/bonus/hypertrophy.

Some fitness circles require a lot of time warming up and stretching. In fact, my circle of training buddies tends to spend 30 minutes to an hour performing activation drills, prehab exercises and rehabilitative exercises before they even touch a barbell. But because some activities, like loaded stretches, can contribute to muscle growth, why not count those towards your total volume? Kit Laughlin's bent-leg hamstring stretch is a staple stretching and hypertrophy exercise in my training arsenal and counts towards my hamstring volume for the week.

You can save time by counting stretches towards your training volume, too.

Tackling Plateaus caused by Not Adhering to the SRA Principle: Poor Rest, Poor Diet and Supplementation

The SRA (stress, recovery, adaptation) principle is the principle that all strength training programs are based off. Truth is, you don't get stronger because of training stress, but because of the recovery and adaptation that happens in response to the training stress. The same is true when the goal is muscle growth.

Recovery comes before adaptation, but recovery doesn't happen inside the gym; it happens outside of it. This means what you do outside of the gym actually has an impact on your gains. Thus, spending hours on end in the gym isn't really going to do you any good if you don't take recovery seriously too. Intense training requires quality rest; otherwise you risk jeopardizing future workouts or even overtraining. In an overtrained or overreached state testosterone levels will drop, muscle growth will come harder, and the risk of injury will increase. As such, make sure you are getting at least 7-8 hours of quality sleep per night – though a meta-analysis published in 2018 by Dr. Daniel Bonnar et al. suggests that sleeping longer, around 9-10 hours of sleep per night, seemed to directly increase athletic performance in athletes from various sports. [2]

Getting quality sleep is not the only thing you can do that has an impact on your recovery, though it may arguably be the most important one. Another key factor to recovery is food intake, which includes both macronutrient and micronutrient intake. If you're interested in adding mass to your body, then you are going to have to increase the number of calories you eat. The law of conservation of mass states that matter cannot be created or destroyed, so the muscle mass you pack onto your body has to come from somewhere – and unsurprisingly, it comes from what you put in your body: food.

To gain mass, you need to be in a caloric surplus. If your goal is to remove mass, you need to be in a caloric deficit. The more you eat, the more fuel you will have for your workouts and the more fuel there is for rebuilding torn muscle fibers when resting. Of course, you can gain muscle mass while being in a caloric deficit and while losing weight too, and it would be my recommendation for most of you reading this book. The benefit of losing weight overall while packing on muscle mass – known as "body recomposition" – is being able to actually *see* your progress, which would do wonders for the principle of consistency. However, too steep of a caloric deficit can also be detrimental to recovery. As such, it may be in your best interest to be in a small caloric deficit, perhaps losing no more than 1-2% of your bodyweight per week, than it is to be in a steep caloric deficit and sacrifice recovery.

Now you can't really talk about building muscle without mentioning protein. Protein helps prevent catabolism, helps with muscle recovery, and increases muscle protein synthesis. Protein is literally the building blocks muscles need to grow; protein is made up of amino acids, and so are muscle tissues and their component cells like actin and myosin. Thus, you must eat adequate amounts of protein if you wish to grow. But how much protein do you need? In October 2013, Dr. Eric Helms et al. published a systematic review that concluded with the range of 2.3-3.1 g of protein per kg of lean body mass as the amount of protein you need to consume when in a caloric deficit. [3] In other words, you need to consume between 1-1.4 g of protein per lb. of lean body mass per day when in a caloric deficit to prevent muscle atrophy.

When not in a caloric deficit, a systematic review and meta-analysis published July 2017 by Dr. Menno Henselmans et al. found no additional benefit to muscle growth and strength when consuming more than 1.62 g of protein per kg of total bodyweight per day, or 0.735 g of protein per lb. of total bodyweight. [4] In layman's terms, eating more protein does not necessarily result in more muscle growth or more strength. Note the differences between the two studies though: The first study I referenced uses *lean body mass* and deals with protein intake when in a caloric deficit, whereas the second uses *total bodyweight* as opposed to lean body mass and deals with caloric surpasses and maintenances states.

Fats are important too. Like how there are essential amino acids, there are also essential fatty acids; but you probably won't get many of the essential fatty acids that you need if you ate only burgers and pizza. Anything considered "essential" means that our bodies need it to function optimally yet can't create. There are many sources of essential fatty acids like borage oil, flaxseed oil, and olive oil, just to name a few. All of these contain fatty acids that are essential to our health, like omega-3, omega-6, omega-7 and omega-9 fatty acids. If you restrict your fat intake too much, it will negatively impact your growth. Why? Fats have a huge impact on your hormonal levels. In fact, the amounts of fats you eat tend to have a direct impact on testosterone levels. As such, fats are not only essential to muscle growth, but they are essential for overall wellbeing.

Micronutrients are also important, especially if you are deficient in any vitamins or minerals. Prolonged vitamin or mineral deficiencies result in serious diseases like scurvy and rickets, which is caused by a Vitamin C and Vitamin D deficiency respectively. Although true vitamin deficiencies are rare, it would be wise to ensure that you consume optimal levels of all 24 essential vitamins and minerals for your body to function at its best. For example, if you're deficient in Vitamin D and Zinc, the latter being lost through sweat, it is very likely that you will not have optimal levels of testosterone – and we all know how important testosterone is for muscle growth. Even a Magnesium deficiency, the second most common deficiency in the western diet after Vitamin D, can affect testosterone levels negatively. As such, it is important to eat a balanced, healthy and varied diet, or alternatively take multivitamins, to ensure that you are consuming enough micronutrients. Some micronutrients, like Magnesium, can even help you sleep better too.

There are also "pseudovitamins" that you can consider supplementing. What is considered a pseudovitamin may vary as it is a nonlegitimate term, but it is often used to describe molecules other than essential vitamins and minerals that are equally as vital for optimal body function. The only difference is that deficiencies in pseudovitamins generally do not result in disease states. However, true creatine deficiency has been shown to result in mental retardation, which can be treated with creatine supplementation if the deficiency is a result of the lack of enzymes to create creatine. (Creatine supplementation will not help if mental retardation is caused by a lack of creatine transport to the brain, though). [5] As such, creatine is often considered a pseudovitamin that also doubles as one of the most proven sports supplements.

If you don't eat animal products, consider supplementing meat-exclusive nutrients such as creatine, beta-alanine and l-carnitine, which is another amino acid and pseudovitamin responsible for alleviating the effects of aging and disease on mitochondria – though it has many other benefits too. L-citrulline, found in many pre-workout supplements for its "pump" effects, is also considered a pseudovitamin to some due to its ability to increase plasma levels of all three dietary amino acids in the urea cycle – arginine, ornithine and citrulline – making it a great all-in-one supplement for cardiovascular and blood flow health.

Maneuvering around Plateaus via the Pursuit of Strength

You should know by now that there is a relationship between size and strength. Increased muscular strength is a result of myofibrillar hypertrophy, which also results in an increase of muscular size. On the other hand, large muscles can make one stronger by creating better leverages for more efficient expressions of strength. As such, if you are struggling to gain size, consider getting stronger. For example, you can take a strength training route and strive to increase your 1RM when it comes to barbell compound exercises. Taking your barbell back squat to 315 lbs., your bench press to 225 lbs., and your deadlift to 405 lbs. can result in some myofibrillar hypertrophy as a byproduct of increased strength.

Oftentimes, people tunnel vision into one very specific goal. Focus is necessary to achieving your goals, but other times it can be even more beneficial to divert your focus elsewhere. Pursuing strength gains when you are struggling to make size gains is one such example. Perhaps you've made a ton of sarcoplasmic hypertrophy gains but made very few myofibrillar hypertrophy gains. Once you start pursuing myofibrillar hypertrophy, you will often find yourself breaking through size plateaus a lot faster than if you were to continue chasing sarcoplasmic hypertrophy. Likewise, if all you've done are contractions like hamstring curls and bicep curls, you may benefit a *lot* from loaded hamstring stretches and biceps stretches to counteract all the tightness developed from contractions. There are always diminishing returns when you pursue any one thing for too long. In fact, many high-level natural powerlifters don't only squat, bench and deadlift, but spend quite a lot of time performing corrective exercises. I have a lot of friends who are being coached by members of Band of Barbells, one of the strongest powerlifting gyms and teams in all of Canada right now, and there is as much focus on corrective exercises as there are for the competition lifts.

Truth is you're only as strong as your weakest link. Real strength isn't measured by how much you squat, bench or deadlift: It's a measure of anything and everything, from your mental toughness to your resilience to injury, to your strength at end range (mobility and flexibility). Thus, try to identify what you can improve on to create a better-rounded you. Taking a step sideways is still a step forward – all you have to do is change your perspective.

Small Details make up the Bigger Picture

One thing that I've learned whilst trying to run a business is that most business owners don't have business problems: Rather, business problems are reflections of their own personal problems. Your business has cash flow problems? You likely have cash flow problems too. Your business is a cluttered mess? You are too. Your business sucks? It's *you* who sucks. I'd wager that this is true for fitness too.

If you're not productive at the gym, you're probably not a very productive person outside the gym either. There was a point in time when my training sessions were no shorter than 3-4 hours, and because of that I accomplished almost nothing outside of the gym other than eating, sleeping and playing video games. As such, it is important to pay attention to the small, little details of life.

If you're hitting plateaus because you aren't adhering to the principle of overload, you probably don't work hard in other areas of life either. To remedy this, try harder in other aspects of life first. And if you're hitting plateaus because you aren't adhering to the principle of consistency, you probably don't commit to other things as well. Start making small commitments to things in everyday life, and over time you may realize that commitment is a lot easier than you think. How you do anything is how you do everything after all, and this is *precisely* why I think taking a principles-approach to training can benefit your life outside the gym.

So, are you a program hopper who jumps between different programs halfway through, or are you someone who finishes what you start? Are you someone who applies what you learn from books, or are you a hoarder of information? Whether you finish this book and apply what you learn or not will say a lot about your other habits in life. Thus, keep reading to learn about the relationship between specificity and exercise selection in Part III.

Part III

Specificity and Exercise Selection

Chapter 15:

Muscle Groups, Muscle Function, Origin and Insertion Points

You should know by now that specificity matters – *a lot*. The principle of specificity is a key principle of muscle growth after all, and the easiest way to fulfill the principle of specificity is with mind-muscle connection to ensure that your muscles are being used. If you're training excruciatingly hard yet fail to see gains, you are most likely neglecting the principle of specificity. Thus, it can be beneficial to have a basic understanding of what each muscle group is responsible for; that way you can train your muscles using movements they're *meant* to perform.

Each muscle and/or muscle group is unique and serves their own unique function. For example, the quadriceps and the hamstrings are both muscles of the thigh, but both serve very different functions. The quadriceps's primary function is knee extension, whereas the hamstrings are responsible for both hip extension and knee flexion. If we know what each muscle and muscle group's primary functions are, we can train them through movements that they're meant to perform – making it that much easier to adhere to the principle of specificity.

Muscle groups are comprised of multiple muscles. The quadriceps, for example, is a series of 4 muscles. Each muscle can also have multiple "heads," and each head can have different origin and insertion points. The origin point is generally closer to the body and doesn't move during contraction. On the other hand, the insertion point is the attachment site that does move when the muscle contracts and is generally further away from the body than the origin point. This is important to know because it helps us identify *how* to train individual muscles.

For example, the superficial chest muscle, the pec major, has 2 heads: the clavicular head and the sternal head. Although both heads insert into the humerus, the bone in your arm that runs from the shoulders to the elbow, the clavicular head originates

Muscle Groups	Functions(s)	Exercise(s)
Abs	Spinal flexion	Crunches, sit-ups, leg raises
Back	Scapular depression and retraction	Horizontal & vertical pulls
Biceps	Elbow flexion	Bicep curls
Calves	Plantar flexion	Calf raises
Chest	Horizontal & incline press	Bench press & incline press
	Horizontal shoulder adduction	Flyes, cable crossovers
Glutes	Hip extension	Hip thrusts, glute bridges
	Hip abduction	Lying hip abductions
Hamstrings	Hip hinge	Deadlifts
	Knee flexion	Hamstring curls
Obliques	Spinal rotation	Side bends, twists
Quads	Knee extension	Squats, lunges, knee extensions
Shoulders	Horizontal shoulder abduction	Rear deltoid flyes
	Shoulder flexion	Vertical press, shoulder raises
	Shoulder abduction	Lateral shoulder raises
Traps	Scapular elevation	Shrugs
Triceps	Elbow extension	Triceps extensions/kickbacks

from the clavicles (the collar bones) while the sternal head originates primarily from the sternum. And since only the insertion point moves during muscle contraction, we can conclude that contracting the pec major is best done by moving our arms relative to both the collar bone and/or chest. However, this is only a rule of thumb; there are some *great* isolation exercises where you move the origin relative to the insertion.

There are a lot of muscles in the body and, because each muscle group is so unique, they can be very difficult to categorize. Thus, I've organized the muscle groups into chapters based on a very popular training split that you've probably heard of: Push/Pull/Legs, also known as PPL for short. Chapter 16 will cover the muscles involved in pushing motions, such as the chest, triceps and anterior deltoid. Chapter 17 will cover the muscles involved in pulling, primarily the upper back, biceps and posterior deltoid. Chapter 18 covers the muscles in the lower body, such as the quadriceps, hamstrings, glutes and calves. Chapter 19 covers miscellaneous muscle groups like the lateral deltoid, upper trapezius muscle fibers, abs and obliques.

Chapter 16 (Push)	Chapter 17 (Pull)	Chapter 18 (Legs)	Chapter 19 (Other)
Chest	Back	Quads	Lateral delt
Triceps	Biceps	Hamstrings	Traps
Anterior delt	Posterior delt	Glutes	Abs/Obliques
		Calves	

Other than the fact that PPL is a very popular bodybuilding training split that most readers of this book will already be familiar with, there are no specific reasons for why I've organized the following chapters this way. Although I could have given each muscle group its own chapter, it would have resulted in very short chapters. As such, feel free to skim through the chapters to find the information you need regarding the muscle groups you are most interested in.

As you will soon see, you probably already know how to best train each muscle group. There aren't any secret training exercises out there that will elicit a lot more growth. Exercises themselves are methods after all, and the impact methods have on building muscle are minuscule compared to properly applying the principles. Thus, don't be surprised if you already know what exercises are best for each muscle group, because what you're likely missing is the proper application of the exercises themselves. However, I'm pretty sure there are some exercises that I will go over that can help you indefinitely.

Chapter 16:

Push Muscles – Training the Chest, Triceps and Anterior Deltoids

There are generally 3 muscle groups involved in any upper body push movement such as the push-up and bench press. These 3 muscle groups are the chest, the triceps and the anterior deltoids. When these muscle groups are developed, your frame will exude masculinity – hence why most "gym bros" put so much emphasis on bench pressing: The bench press develops *all* the pushing muscles. As such, you can always expect to have a compound pressing movement in your training program.

Training the Chest

The chest is made up of 2 muscles, the pectoralis major and the pectoralis minor. When you think of a thick, wide chest you are thinking of a developed pec major, as it lays superficial to the pec minor. The pec minor, although important for scapular stabilization and downward scapular rotation, is often invisible to the naked eye. As such, growing the chest is often synonymous to growing the pec major. Nonetheless, the pec minor does get trained indirectly in many upper back exercises – so direct training for the pec minor is oftentimes unnecessary.

The pec major has two heads – the clavicular head and the sternal, or sternocostal, head – both of which insert into the humerus. To train the pec major, you will need to perform horizontal and incline pressing movements. The sternal head is used more extensively in horizontal presses, while the clavicular head sees more use in incline presses. Chest isolation exercises, like flyes and crossovers, are also great at training the chest as it removes the other 2 muscle groups that are used extensively when pressing: the triceps and the anterior deltoids. In fact, I'd wager that you often see greater chest activation and contraction with chest isolation exercises than you will with compounds. Why? Because isolation exercises like cable crossovers train the chest through one of its primary movement functions: horizontal shoulder adduction – which is the bringing of your arms across your body towards your midline. And the further you bring your arms across your chest, the more work the pecs are doing.

As such, there are 3 movements that you must incorporate for training the chest: horizontal presses, incline presses and chest isolation exercises. Both horizontal and incline presses, such as the flat bench press and the incline bench press respectively, are important as the chest is a prime mover in pressing movements. Whereas horizontal presses stress the sternal head, incline presses train the clavicular head – but only up to a certain point: An incline steeper than 45 degrees shifts a lot of emphasis onto the anterior deltoids. Most pressing exercises will be compound movements involving more than just the chest, so it is a good idea to incorporate chest isolation exercises too, like the cable crossover, to ensure adequate chest stimulation.

Of course, using mind-muscle connection to ensure that your chest is the prime mover in pressing compounds is an option over the strength training approach of being as efficient as possible with the lift. In fact, performing flat bench presses with your feet up on the bench has been shown to increase muscle activation for all pressing muscles, including the triceps and shoulders. [1] (As a safety precaution, note that this is an extremely inefficient way to bench press, and that you most definitely *won't* be able to press as much weight as you do with a regular bench press.) Another option to increasing specificity is to perform presses with cables and machines. Pressing using cables so that your hands are super close together when your elbows are fully extended can result in a *lot* of chest activation because it incorporates horizontal shoulder adduction into the pressing motion.

Training the Triceps

The triceps is a three-headed muscle that makes up the back of the upper arm and is used extensively in all pressing movements – whether horizontal, vertical, upside down, or any angle in between. This is because the triceps brachii (its full name) is the primary mover of elbow extension, which is the locking out of your arms.

Your triceps will generally be the first muscle group to fatigue during compound pressing and pushing exercises, mainly because of their smaller size relative to the other muscle groups. This smaller size means less muscle glycogen storages. Also, the triceps tend to also have the highest ratio of type II muscle fibers to type I muscle fibers as well, meaning it is powerful and explosive but very vulnerable to fatigue. Hence why it is so important to incorporate chest isolation exercises for chest growth: Without isolation movements for your chest, your chest development will be severely limited by the endurance of your triceps.

All three heads of the triceps insert into the ulna, which is one of two bones in your forearm. Two of the heads – the lateral and medial heads – originate from the humerus, while the remaining head – the long head – originates from the scapula and aids in shoulder extension as well. Direct triceps training in the form of triceps extensions will train all heads adequately, but the long head can be emphasized more using overhead triceps extensions or skull crushers. While the long head is the largest and strongest of the three triceps heads, the lateral head is responsible for the coveted horseshoe-look of well-developed arms. As such, you may want to include triceps pushdowns using a rope, pronating your arm at extension, to emphasize and grow your horseshoe. On the other hand, if you want to emphasize the medial head, perform underhand triceps extensions with a straight bar. Though most triceps exercises will grow both the lateral and medial heads of the triceps, my horseshoe never really took shape until I started doing pushdowns with a rope.

Training the Anterior Deltoid

The anterior deltoid, one of 3 heads of the shoulder, is used extensively in pressing motions – whether horizontal, incline, vertical or upside-down. The anterior deltoids are largely responsible for shoulder flexion. Shoulder flexion involves moving your arms up in front of you and overhead; hence why anterior shoulder raises and overhead presses are the exercises of choice for training the anterior deltoids. Failure to incorporate both movements means that you aren't taking the anterior deltoids through its full range of motion. All the deltoid muscles originate from their attachment to the scapula and the clavicle, and all insert into the humerus.

However, whether you need direct anterior deltoid training is questionable. Dr. Mike Israetel, an elite bodybuilder and bodybuilding coach, suggests that the horizontal pressing you perform to build your chest may already stress the anterior deltoids enough to stimulate muscle growth. [2] Even Glenn Pendlay, a Level-5 USA Weightlifting Coach and perhaps one of the most well-known American weightlifting coaches around, favors the bench press over the overhead press for strength development – which is surprising as the sport of Olympic Weightlifting always involves putting hundreds of pounds overhead. According to Pendlay, the overhead press was only used if beginner Olympic weightlifting athletes had trouble getting the barbell locked out over and behind the head; otherwise the bench press was the go-to exercise for shoulder development. [3]

Although overhead pressing was popularized again through many strength training programs like Starting Strength, StrongLifts and even Jim Wendler's 5/3/1, you probably don't need direct anterior deltoid training if you are already benching for chest development. Even I tell strength trainees who are interested in powerlifting to swap out their overhead presses for a bench press variation like the close-grip bench press. Overhead presses tend to plateau much faster than any other compound lift, whereas the bench press doesn't plateau as fast and trains the same muscles but with a heavier load... so why not just bench press instead if your goal is powerlifting or muscle growth? Of course, this is assuming that you are performing compound pressing movements, like bench presses and incline presses, for chest development. If your chest training involves no compound pressing movements, consider including overhead presses into your training to stimulate anterior deltoid growth.

Chapter 17:

Pull Muscles – Training the Upper Back, Biceps and Posterior Deltoids

The pushing muscles get all the attention, primarily because a wide chest, broad shoulders and large arms exude masculinity. However, when the pull muscles – the upper back, biceps and posterior deltoids – are undertrained and weak relative to the push muscles, you will end up slouching; and slouching is *not* a good look. As such, it is important to take upper back training seriously, though few people do. And often, those will do take upper back training seriously are doing it *wrong*: They use their arms way too much when performing pulling exercises, which defeats the whole purpose of back training in the first place. According to the principle of specificity, if you are trying to train your back, use your back – not your arms.

Training All of the Muscles in the Upper Back

The upper back is comprised of so many different, individual muscles that it seems silly to group them all together, but there is a good reason to do it: Almost *all* of the muscles in the upper back can be trained through the combination of two movement patterns – vertical pulling and horizontal pulling.

But first, let's cover what muscles are in the upper back. The largest muscle located in the upper back is the latissimus dorsi, or "lat" muscles for short, which originates primarily from the spine and inserts into the humerus. Well-developed lats help accentuate your V-taper, which is a coveted and aesthetic look based on the width of your shoulders relative to the width of your waist. The trapezius muscles, also known as the traps, are also located on the upper back, though the upper region of the trapezius muscle is generally trained separately from all the others. Lastly, the rhomboid muscles and teres major can be found in the upper back too but lie underneath superficial muscles like the traps.

As stated earlier, almost all the muscles located in the upper back can be trained using horizontal and vertical pulling movements such as rows and pull-ups. And this is especially true for the lats, which are used extensively in reaching and pulling movements. Rows train the middle and lower regions of the traps, as well as the rhomboids. The teres major muscle, which is responsible for pulling the arms downwards and rotating the arms inwards, sees a lot of stimulation from horizontal and vertical pulls – despite it not being its primary function. If you want to isolate the teres major, you can do so with straight-arm pulldowns. Regardless, training the upper back can be better thought of as performing as many pulling exercises and variations as possible. Isolating and training the individual muscles in the upper back makes no sense as all the muscles in the upper back work together as one functional unit.

Horizontal pulls, like barbell and machine rows, train the lats, the rhomboids and the mid traps. However, there are 2 key things you *must* do when performing rows in order to incorporate the rhomboids and mid traps. First off, incorporating the mid traps into your upper back training requires retracting the scapula as you pull, because the mid trap's primary function is scapular retraction. Additionally, incorporating the rhomboids into horizontal pulls require squeezing and contracting the mid back during the concentric. Failure to do any of the 2 will result in a lot more arm involvement and a lot less back involvement, which is bad for growing the upper back. Unfortunately, most people suck at the former – retracting their scapula – me included. As such I've found it beneficial to perform horizontal shrugs on a seated cable row machine as, according to independent researcher Chris Beardsley, they are one of the best ways to isolate and train scapular retraction. [1] Performing horizontal shrugs before other horizontal pulling movements will help you retract your scapulae and recruit your back muscles.

Vertical pulls, such as pull-ups, train the lats and the lower traps, but getting proper lower trap training requires scapular depression. Before you start performing a pull-up, depress your scapula first. This will push out your chest and helps involve the teres major muscle too. Like executing horizontal pulls properly, performing vertical pulls without your scapula depressed will result in more arm involvement and less back involvement.

Training the Biceps

The biceps muscle is a two-headed muscle that makes up the front of the upper arm, and it is responsible for elbow flexion and forearm supination. Elbow flexion can be defined as the curling motion of the arm, executed at the elbow joint; hence why direct biceps training will always involve biceps curls. Forearm supination is the rotating of your hand so that your palms are facing upwards and to the sky. Since the chin-up uses a supinated grip, it has *slightly* more biceps involvement than the pull-up. But despite all the attention the biceps get, size-wise the biceps only make up about one-third of the arm whereas the triceps make up the remaining two-thirds.

There are two additional muscles located on the anterior of the humerus that assist the biceps. The first one is the coracobrachialis, which flexes the arm near the shoulder joint and aids the chest in horizontal shoulder adduction. Thus, when you perform dumbbell flyes you may feel the load in your upper arm as well. The second, and perhaps one of the most overlooked muscles in the upper arm, is the brachialis. The brachialis originates from the middle of the humerus and inserts into the ulna, making it the prime mover of elbow flexion and the strongest elbow flexor in the human body – *much* stronger than the biceps. When developed, the brachialis is responsible for making the upper arm look thick from the front, hence why it is sometimes referred to as the "lower bicep" or the "outer bicep."

Pulling exercises generally involve some biceps recruitment, but direct biceps training is mandatory if you want to stimulate bicep growth. As such, make sure you incorporate curls into your training regime. The brachialis will be trained through curls too, but it is only fully activated when the arm is flexing but not moving. Although you should always be contracting the muscles you are training to ensure activation, squeezing your biceps hard during the concentric contraction is the only way to grow the brachialis – making it that much more important for bicep growth. To get a feeling of what brachialis activation feels like, perform a curl right now and contract as hard as you can. You should feel the part of your biceps closest to the elbow joint flexing the hardest. That's the brachialis at play. As such, make sure you train the brachialis for complete upper arm development. This means squeezing your biceps hard at contraction (though you should be doing that for every exercise you do anyways).

However, there is another key takeaway regarding biceps training: The biceps brachii is more responsible for forearm supination than it is elbow flexion, mainly because the brachialis is such a strong elbow flexor. Thus, make sure you perform your curls with as much forearm supination as possible. You can do this by 1) starting your curls with your hands in a pronated position; 2) twisting and pointing your thumbs out as much as possible during the concentric contraction; or 3) a combination of both techniques.

Training the Posterior Deltoid

The posterior deltoid is one of 3 heads of the shoulder muscle, making up the back of the shoulder, with a responsibility for shoulder extension. Shoulder extension, also known as horizontal shoulder abduction, is the pulling of your arms back behind your body, followed by the squeezing of the shoulder blades together.

If you're performing horizontal pulls and rows properly, you shouldn't need a ton of direct posterior deltoid training. That's because, like the rhomboids and mid trap, you can train the posterior deltoids using rows. However, if your posterior deltoids are lacking relative to the anterior deltoids (and they are for most of the population), it may be a good idea to include direct posterior deltoid training. You can incorporate posterior deltoid training directly, through exercises like face pulls or rear deltoid flyes, or indirectly, through slight modifications to the exercises you use to train your lateral deltoids. For more information regarding the latter, check out the section on training the lateral deltoids in Chapter 19.

Chapter 18:

Leg Muscles – Training the Quads, Hamstrings, Glutes and Calves

People often hate training legs because of the soreness that follows. But the legs include some of the biggest muscles in the body, which means training just the legs alone can result in a huge hormonal response that can rival training multiple other body parts simultaneously. As such, training the lower body can indirectly result in better upper body growth, primarily through elevated testosterone levels.

Fortunately, there is a way to combat the delayed-onset muscle soreness (DOMS) involved with leg training, which is what scares people away from leg day in the first place. All you need to do is increase lower body training frequency, and your body will adapt accordingly. This is known as the repeated bout effect. In fact, Olympic weightlifters often squat multiple times a week. Not because they're masochists; they've just adapted to lower body training and don't experience DOMS anymore.

Training the Quads

The quadriceps are a series of 4 muscles – the rectus femoris, the vastus lateralis, the vastus intermedius and the vastus medialis – that make up the anterior of your femurs, which are the largest and strongest bones in the human body. Three of the 4 heads of the quadriceps originate from the femur while the rectus femoris originates from deep inside the hip socket and from the front of the spine, making it a hip flexor too. All heads insert into the kneecap in one way or another, generally via inserting into a tendon near the knee that merges into the kneecap. If you guessed that extending your knee contracts the quads, you'd be correct: The quads are primarily responsible for knee extension, which is the locking out of the knees.

Squats are some of the best quad developers out there due to the range of motion the knee goes through in a squat. However, know that you don't have to squat ass-to-grass, as tension is removed from the quads at certain knee angles. This angle varies depending on the individual, as well as whether you are performing front squats, Olympic-style high-bar squats or powerlifting-style low-bar squats. As such, partial squats like box squats may be superior for quad development as it allows you to maintain tension on the quads. If you're a powerlifter or Olympic weightlifter though, continue squatting deep as partial squats may not be relevant for your sport.

The leg press is viable for quad development too. However, even though I'm built for squatting, my favorite quad exercise is the lunge. The lunge is a unilateral movement with a ton of variations, and it also doubles as a hip flexor opener. In fact, the best quad and hip flexor stretches are generally lunge variants themselves. Do note that, as a unilateral movement where you work one leg at a time, the lunge is inherently unstable compared to bilateral movements like the squat and leg press. This makes it that much easier to accidentally load a ton of pressure onto the knees, which can result in some pretty bad knee pain.

Training the Hamstrings

The hamstrings are a series of 3 muscles – the semitendinosus, the semimembranosus, and the biceps femoris, which has a short and long head. All 3 muscles originate from the pelvic, except for the short head of the biceps femoris which originates from the femur. Both heads of the biceps femoris merge and have an insertion point on the head of the fibula, while the semitendinosus and the semimembranosus have an insertion point on the tibia. The fibula and the tibia are the two bones that make up your lower leg.

All of the muscles that make up the hamstring are responsible for extending the hip. You can train hip extension using hip hinge exercises like tire flips and deadlifts. Although there may be some hinging of the hip in exercises like the squat and barbell row, these exercises do not extend the hip through its full range of motion. As such, you can expect to have deadlifts in your training arsenal all the time. Personally, I love performing single-legged Romanian deadlifts as an activation exercise, with a resistance band wrapped around my knees to ensure proper knee tracking.

Perform these supported – meaning hold onto something for balance so that you can focus on engaging the hamstrings – and with either a dumbbell or kettlebell in your other hand.

The hamstring muscles – bar the short head of the biceps femoris – are also responsible for knee flexion, which is the bending of the leg at the knee joint. A prime example of knee flexion is hamstring curls. As such, try to include knee flexion exercises in your training to round out overall hamstring development.

Training the Glutes

The gluteal muscles, or glutes, are a series of 3 muscles: the gluteus maximus, the gluteus medius and the gluteus minimus. The glutes are used extensively in lower body compound movements, such as squats and deadlifts. And according to Dr. Mike Israetel, if you're already performing heavy squats you probably won't need direct glute work to grow the glutes. [1]

However, I am going to side with Dr. Bret Contreras and tell you that you *need* direct glute training. As a strength athlete myself, I am no stranger to heavy squats and deadlifts. Yet, weak glutes are perhaps one of the most common causes of pain and injury for me and my circle of powerlifters and strength enthusiasts. Why? Because squats and deadlifts do not train the glutes much; people are often able to contract their glutes harder during bodyweight glute activation drills than they are able to during max squat or deadlift attempts. [2] In other words, squats and deadlifts aren't specific exercises for the glutes and shouldn't be counted as glute work.

The gluteus maximus is the largest muscle in the entire body in terms of mass, whose main function is hip extension. Hip extension, or the straightening of the hip joint, is evident in glute exercises like barbell hip thrusts. Although hip extension happens in almost every lower body compound exercise, the strongest contraction is always felt in exercises that isolate the glutes, such as hip thrusts.

The gluteus medius and gluteus minimus, sometimes referred to as the lateral glutes, are similarly shaped muscles with similar functions: Both are prime movers in hip abduction, which is the moving of your legs out and away from your midline. Thus, any sort of movement where you are pushing your knees out will tend to train the glute medius and glute minimus, including lying hip abductions, lateral walks, and squat variations like squatting with a resistance band around your legs. Even locomotion exercises that move in the lateral plane can work. However, I often find myself defaulting to kettlebell swings for glute work as, when done properly, they can be a quick and effective way of restoring glute and hip function.

Training the Calves

The calves are made up of two muscles, the gastrocnemius and the soleus, which are both responsible for plantar flexion. Plantar flexion can be thought of as raising the heel or pressing the ball of your foot downwards, but which calf muscle is primarily responsible for plantar flexion depends on the position of your legs. When your legs are bent as if you were seated, the soleus is more actively engaged than the gastrocnemius. On the other hand, if your legs are straight and locked out as if you were standing, plantar flexion can largely be attributed to the gastrocnemius. As such, make sure you incorporate both seated and standing calf raises in your training routine; though I would favor standing calf raises due to the gastrocnemius being a much bigger muscle than the soleus.

Chapter 19:

Other Muscles – Training the Lateral Deltoids, Traps, Abs and Obliques

There are other muscle groups that don't really play a part in pushing, pulling, or lower body movements. These muscles include the lateral deltoid, upper traps and the superficial muscles of the core such as the abs and obliques. Although they don't participate in PPL movement patterns, they should still be trained if your goal is overall muscle development. Having a balanced and aesthetic body is key when it comes to winning bodybuilding competitions or just looking good.

Training the Lateral Deltoid

The lateral deltoid is the last of the 3 heads of the shoulder. Since it is located on the outside of the shoulder, once developed the lateral deltoids will broaden your upper body. Responsible for shoulder abduction, which is the raising of your arms outwards to the side of your body, the lateral deltoids are trained primarily through lateral shoulder raises and upright rows. In fact, an upright row is literally the same movement as a lateral shoulder raise but with elbows bent – which creates a shorter moment arm that allows the use of heavier loads.

It is possible to train both the lateral deltoids and the posterior deltoids using slight modifications of the same exercises: Bending over ever so slightly when performing lateral shoulder raises will shift some of the load onto the posterior deltoids. Performing lateral shoulder raises when you're fully bent over will target the posterior deltoids almost exclusively, while performing them upright will train the lateral deltoids exclusively.

Unlike the anterior and posterior deltoids, the lateral deltoid is rarely used during compounds movements. Thus, I highly recommend direct training for the lateral deltoids. Because let's face it, who wouldn't want to have wider shoulders? I often perform lateral deltoid work on my push days to complement the other beach body muscles involved in pushing compounds. My exercise of choice is the Olympic weightlifting Klokov press, also known as the behind-the-neck snatch-grip overhead press. Note that this is *not* an easy exercise and will require a *ton* of mobility, and I probably wouldn't recommend it unless you have a good snatch position or are an advanced lifter (and even then I would recommend starting with just the barbell). So why am I telling you about the Klokov press? Because I have yet to find an exercise that can match the pump my upper traps, lateral, and posterior deltoids get from the Klokov press. If you are an Olympic weightlifter or have very healthy and flexible shoulders, I would give it a try. Otherwise, I highly recommend upright rows using a rope, which removes a lot of the dangers that come with upright rowing a barbell.

Training the Upper Traps

The upper traps, sometimes referred to as the superior region or the upper trap fibers, are the prime movers in scapular elevation. There aren't many exercises that involve scapular elevation other than shrugs themselves. And like the lateral deltoids, the upper traps aren't trained in compound exercises that involve the mid and lower traps. Thus, when people talk about training the traps, they're almost always talking about training the upper trap fibers.

However, whether you need direct trap training in order to grow your upper traps is questionable. Holding onto anything heavy – whether it is a heavy barbell during deadlifts, a heavy dumbbell for one-armed rows, or even famer's carries with heavy suitcases – requires a lot of isometric upper trap activation in order to hold your scapula in place. In fact, most powerlifters and strongman competitors have huge upper traps despite rarely ever performing shrugs; their traps grow as a byproduct of all the deadlifts and carries they perform.

Dr. Mike Israetel suggests avoiding direct trap training in the form of shrugs if you're already doing heavy pulls. This is because excessive shrugging can cause tendon pain – often in your biceps. [1] If you intend on performing shrugs, do them on your pull day for complete upper back development. More importantly, perform shrugs on a barbell and with a wide grip. Why? For peak contraction to happen in the traps, your arms should be in line with the muscle fibers of the upper traps – which run diagonal, not up and down. Try it yourself: Perform a shrug with your arms by your side, and then another with your arms at about 30° from your body; you'll notice a better contraction in your traps with your arms out at an angle. The wider grip used in Klokov presses is what makes them so effective at growing the traps, too.

Training the Abs and Obliques

The abs are perhaps one of the most popular muscles. Heck, everyone wants them. If you're already lean, training the abs will help them pop. Otherwise, you may not need direct abdominal training. That's because heavy compounds that require your body to carry around excessive external load, like a 600 lb. back squat for example, will stimulate growth in your core, and subsequently your abs. This is why powerlifters and strongman competitors tend to have big, muscular guts: Training the abs, whether directly or indirectly (by walking out a 600 lb. squat for example), *will* grow them. Thus, if you want to compete in physique, it may be a bad idea to train your abs as it may hurt your V-taper.

But if you're already relatively lean and still can't see your abs, the muscle you'd want to train is the rectus abdominis, which is the prime mover in spinal flexion. Spinal flexion, the bringing of your legs and spine closer together, is very evident in popular abdominal exercises like sit-ups, crunches and hanging leg raises. The muscle located to the sides of the rectus abdominis is the (external) oblique and, as the prime mover in spinal rotation, it can be trained with side twists.

Since you're probably already going to be using your core on lower body days, abdominal exercises at the end of the workout can ensure that your abs and obliques are overloaded. Note that there are core strengthening exercises that will not grow your abs, such as the bird-dog exercise, as the load (your bodyweight) is not enough to stimulate growth. As such, even if your goal is to maintain a slim waist, it can be a good idea to perform core strengthening exercises occasionally. In fact, a weak core is often the root cause of lower back pain.

Conclusion

Maybe you were struggling to build muscle, despite spending hours and hours at the gym or hundreds of dollars on supplements per month. If you *were* able to slap on quality muscle, you probably didn't put on as much muscle as you'd hoped. You probably felt that others were either juicing or had top-tier genetics. Regardless, you were searching for information – otherwise you wouldn't have stumbled onto this book. And if you're like most people, this probably wasn't the first book on muscle growth that you've purchased. How do I know? Because I've been there myself.

The fitness industry has turned building muscle into a complicated science. If you ever wanted to build muscle according to the fitness industry, you had to have the ideal meal frequency, eat at very specific times, be taking their newest supplements, train with the perfect combination of volume, frequency, and intensity, and top it all off with their secret training method. But, in reality, all you needed were to understand the principles – not be sold more and more methods. It's no wonder why so many people struggle to pack on muscle mass in this day and age.

Truth is there are no secrets to muscle growth. There aren't any secret exercises, training methods or supplements. Most supplements don't even have solid scientific backing. The things that do work – like training hard, being consistent and utilizing mind-muscle connection – are tried and true. But the fitness industry can't market hard work as fun and exciting; people want shortcuts after all. If the fitness industry told you to be consistent with your training, they'd lose out on the opportunity to sell you their latest and greatest programs. Although there may be exercises that can potentially isolate muscle groups better than the others, these exercises aren't secret innovations in training but basic human anatomy.

You knew everything there was to building muscle, but you never had the confidence to act on it. But things have changed now... For you, this is the end of looking for new information. It is also the end of hoarding information, because knowing more than the next guy isn't a principle of muscle growth. In fact, the principles of muscle growth are applications, not knowledge. It's about applying what you know and doing it with consistency and utmost intensity.

For you, this is a new beginning. Not only is it one where you make gains, but it is the beginning of a new life – because principles apply there too. Once you start working hard in the gym, it will carry over to other aspects of your life. The same can be said about consistency. Once you get into a habit of going to the gym you will slowly fall into a routine that integrates fitness habits into your lifestyle. You know all this already – you've read this book, after all – but knowing is only half the battle. So, get your butt into the gym and do some work.

ANDY XIONG

Bonus:

Creating Your Own Muscle Building Program in 3 Simple Steps

Note: You can get a PDF/printout of this chapter, an enlarged copy of the sample 5-day program, and more at www.andyxiong.com/bonus/hypertrophy.

Often, people think that programming is complicated. For performance sports that require periodization, it may be true. But for muscle growth, programming is as easy as 1-2-3. Following the principles-based training protocol provided in Chapter 5, you can come up with a program tailored for muscle growth almost instantly! Here's how you can create a personalized training program specifically for muscle growth in 3 simple steps.

Step 1. Decide how often you want to train

Showing up is half the battle; and one of the worst ways to fail is to not show up in the first place. Thus, if you want to build muscle, *you must show up on all your training days.* The principle of consistency is a key principle of muscle growth, after all. And in order to combat the fact that you might skip training days, *you* should dictate how frequently *you* want to train. That way, you won't have anyone to blame but yourself if you are ever inconsistent with your training.

Often, people think that they need a very high training frequency in order to build muscle, but that's not the case. As explained in Chapter 6, training frequency can be as low as twice a week. This is because a training frequency of two times a week allows you to hit both the optimal minimum weekly volume *and* the optimal volume per training session, as observed in Chapter 8. So, the question is: How often do *you* want to train? Below is a table of how a week of training will look like, based on *your* preferred training frequency:

TRAINING DAYS						
FREQ.	M	T	W	T	F	S
2x/week	FULL			FULL		
3x/week	FULL		UPPER		LOWER	
4x/week	UPPER	LOWER		UPPER	LOWER	
5x/week	UPPER	LOWER		PUSH	PULL	LEGS
6x/week	PUSH	PULL	LEGS	PUSH	PULL	LEGS

Though, assuming your goal is to *maximize* muscle growth, you would train differently if you were training twice a week than if you were training 6 times a week. You want your weekly training volume to be equal regardless of how frequently (or infrequently) you decide to train. Volume per session and frequency have an inverse relationship – meaning the fewer training days you want, the more volume you need to perform per workout. Using the minimum volume recommendation of 10 sets per week, your training sessions will be populated according to your ideal training frequency as follows:

TRAINING SESSIONS					
Muscle Group	Full	Upper	Lower	Push	Pull	Legs
Chest	5 sets	5 sets		5 sets		
Back	5 sets	5 sets			5 sets	
Biceps	5 sets	5 sets			5 sets	
Triceps	5 sets	5 sets		5 sets		
Delt (Post)	5 sets	5 sets			5 sets	
Delt (Lat)	5 sets	5 sets		5 sets		
Delt (Ant)	0-5 sets	0-5 sets		0-5 sets		
Traps	0-5 sets	0-5 sets			0-5 sets	
Abs	0-5 sets		0-5 sets			0-5 sets
Glutes	0-5 sets		0-5 sets			0-5 sets
Quads	5 sets		5 sets			5 sets
Hamstrings	5 sets		5 sets			5 sets
Calves	5 sets		5 sets			5 sets

So, if you were to train twice a week, you'd have to perform 2 full body workouts in order to match the training volume of someone performing a Push/Pull/Legs workout 6 times a week. Each full body training session would consist of a minimum of 45 sets, whereas each Push/Pull/Legs session would consist of a minimum of 15 sets. Of course, that is only if your goal is to maximize muscle growth; otherwise, you don't need to train 10 sets per week per muscle group. You can always opt to forego training some muscle groups that you have no intention of growing, train using lower volumes (like 5 sets per muscle group per week), or train using primarily compound exercises to shorten your workout as discussed in Chapter 14. But know that volume is the primary driver of muscle growth – and your results will reflect the levels of training volume you perform.

Step 2. Choose your exercises

Now that you have an idea of how a week of training will look like, it is time to figure out what each training session will look like. This is where things can get a bit more complicated, solely because of the number of variables that you can manipulate. Although weekly volume and sets per training session have been determined, training variables like the number of repetitions, intensity, load, and exercises still need to be defined.

Fortunately, we have already covered what the ideal rep ranges, intensities and loads are. As a reminder: In order to satisfy the principle of overload, a key principle of muscle growth, you will train using as-many-reps-as-possible (AMRAP) sets, as explained in Chapter 7. AMRAP sets imply high intensity training, and with variable loads. Refer to Chapter 9 for more information about training intensity and load, and why intensity matters much more than load. If you have experience using an RPE scale, you can use that instead.

For exercise selection, you want to perform exercises that your muscles are meant to perform in order to strengthen adherence to the principle of specificity. This was covered in Chapters 16 to 19. The table below summarizes the different muscle groups, their various functions and examples of exercises that train each muscle group:

Chest

Horizontal press	Barbell/dumbbell bench press
Incline press	Incline barbell/dumbbell press
Horizontal shoulder adduction	Cable crossovers, flyes

Back

Horizontal pull	Barbell/dumbbell/cable rows
Vertical pull	Pull-ups, lat/straight-arm pulldowns

Biceps

Elbow flexion	Biceps curls (supinated grip)

Triceps

Elbow extension	Triceps extensions, triceps kickbacks
	Overhead triceps extensions

Posterior Deltoid

Horizontal shoulder abduction	Face pulls, rear delt flyes

Lateral Deltoid

Shoulder abduction	Upright rows, lateral delt raises

Anterior Deltoid

Shoulder flexion	Overhead/military/dumbbell press
	Anterior shoulder raises

Traps

Scapular elevation	Barbell/dumbbell shrugs

Abs

Spinal flexion	Crunches, sit-ups, leg raises
Spinal rotation	Side twists

Glutes

Hip extension	Hip thrusts, glute bridges
Hip flexion	Lying hip abductions

Quads

Knee extension	Squats, leg press, lunges
Hip extension	Squats, lunges

Hamstrings

Hip hinge	Conventional/Romanian deadlifts
Knee flexion	Hamstring curls, Nordic curls

Calves

Plantar flexion	Standing calf raises
	Seated calf raises

Note that some muscle groups are best trained using compound movements. The quadriceps, for example, is best trained using squats because squats incorporate both knee extension and hip flexion at great ranges of motion. However, you do not have to take a strength training approach when performing your compounds, as explained in Chapter 7.

When it comes to exercise selection, there are some nitty-gritty details to keep in mind. For example, what angle is most optimal for the incline bench press? Why are overhead presses – or direct anterior deltoid training – unnecessary in the first place? As such, here are some considerations for each muscle group:

Chest
> Though horizontal and incline pressing movements are some of the best exercises to build your pectorals, never underestimate how much isolation exercises like cable crossovers can impact your physique. If your triceps are bigger than your pecs, it's a sign that you should incorporate more isolation work for your chest!
>
> For incline presses, keep the angle between 30-45° to prevent shifting too much load onto the anterior deltoids.
>
> For a bodyweight or calisthenics chest isolation exercise that

rivals even cable crossovers in chest activation, check out *[Bodyweight Workouts: How to Program for Fast Muscle Growth using Calisthenics Hypertrophy Training](#)*.

Back

Although the entire upper back can be trained using horizontal and vertical pulling movements exclusively, there should be a slight preference for horizontal pulling movements due to its shoulder health properties. I get it though, pull-ups are cool. But healthy shoulders that seem to defy the stresses of aging? Even cooler.

Biceps

One of the greatest complaints is the biceps looking small from the front. That's not the biceps though – it's the brachialis! Despite it not being one of the two heads of the biceps, this muscle can still be trained through curls – if you squeeze your biceps *hard* during each rep. And because the brachialis is such a strong elbow flexor, make sure to incorporate forearm supination into your curls to help isolate your biceps.

Triceps

Make sure you incorporate triceps pushdowns with a rope. Why? Refer to Chapter 16. Triceps kickbacks often provide the best triceps activation, so they make a great exercise to either start or end your triceps training with.

Posterior Deltoid

Highly recommend face pulls for shoulder health and rhomboid growth. Rear deltoid flyes are generally better at growing the posterior deltoids, though.

Lateral Deltoid

Lateral shoulder flyes and upright rows can cause pain for a lot of individuals. To remedy this, try looping a resistance band over your traps to keep your scapula down when performing lateral deltoid exercises.

Anterior Deltoid

As covered in Chapter 16, some of the best coaches in the world have the opinion that overhead/military presses are unnecessary – for both bodybuilding *and* strength purposes. As such, training the anterior deltoids directly is completely optional. But if you're not performing *any* compound pressing movements at all, opt to incorporate some overhead pressing.

Traps

You use your traps a lot. Thus, training the traps directly isn't necessary. And as explained in Chapter 19, too much shrugging can be harmful.

Abs

Optional unless you are trying to *grow* your abs. Core and ab strengthening exercises are important though.

Glutes

Optional as direct training is not needed to grow the glutes, but I highly recommend direct glute work. See Chapter 18 for why. Personally, I have been enjoying kettlebell swings a lot as it incorporates all the gluteal muscles.

Quads

Though leg presses and knee extensions are viable exercises for growing the quads, your quadriceps training should favor compounds such as squats and lunges as they incorporate both hip flexion and knee extension.

Hamstrings

Your training should slightly favor hip hinging exercises like deadlifts since all the hamstring muscles are involved in the hip hinge movement pattern.

Calves

Slightly favor standing calf raises due to the gastrocnemius muscle being a bigger and more superficial muscle than the soleus.

Neck & Forearms

You shouldn't need direct neck and forearm training. But if you forgo heavy compounds like the deadlift or want full body growth, consider reading *Bodyweight Workouts: How to Program for Fast Muscle Growth using Calisthenics Hypertrophy Training* as the best neck and forearm exercises are calisthenics exercises.

After choosing what exercises you want to perform, you'll find that your program is fully populated and ready. If you're too lazy to choose your own exercises and piece together your own program, I provide a 5-day training template below. Why a 5-day training program? Not because it is superior; but because giving you a 5-day training template allows you to reuse the upper body, lower body, push, pull and/or leg days for your very own 4-day or 6-day program! That's like giving you 3 programs at once – a 4-day one, a 5-day one and a 6-day one.

SAMPLE 5-DAY PROGRAM

Monday – Upper Body

   Chest Superset:
   2 sets   Barbell bench press
   2 sets   Barbell rows
   Back Superset:
   2 sets   Seated rows
   1 set   Pull-ups
   Upper Body – Single Sets:
   2 sets   Face pulls
   5 sets   Upright rows
   2 sets   Triceps kickback
   5 sets   Biceps curls
   3 sets   Triceps extensions
   Cable Superset:
   3 sets   Cable crossovers
   3 sets   Rear delt flyes

Tuesday – Lower Body

   Activation:
   2 sets   Kettlebell swings
   Lower Body – Single Sets:
   2 sets   Squats
   3 sets   Lunges
   3 sets   Hip thrusts
   Hamstring Superset:
   2 sets   Romanian deadlifts
   2 sets   Hamstring curls
   Calf Superset:
   3 sets   Standing calf raises
   2 sets   Seated calf raises

Thursday - Push

   Push – Single Sets:
   2 sets   Overhead press
   1 set   Incline bench press
   1 set   Dumbbell bench

2 sets Upright rows
3 sets Cable crossovers
Shoulder Superset:
3 sets Lateral deltoid raises
3 sets Anterior deltoid raises

Friday – Pull

Pull – Single Sets:
1 set   Pendlay row
2 sets Lat pulldown
2 sets Seated rows
3 sets Barbell curls
2 sets Dumbbell curls
3 sets Face pulls
2 sets Rear delt flyes

Saturday – Legs

Activation:
2 sets Kettlebell swings
Legs – Single Sets:
2 sets Squats
3 sets Lunges
Hamstring Superset:
2 sets Romanian deadlifts
2 sets Hamstring curls
Calf Superset:
3 sets Standing calf raises
2 sets Seated calf raises

Please visit www.andyxiong.com/bonus/hypertrophy for a better, more visual printout, as well as notes.

However, there's still one more super important step – *and that's actually doing the program.* For most of you this will be the hardest step, but it's also the step that separates the muscular and aesthetic from the weak and scrawny.

Step 3. Execute your training program

As much as you think having the perfect training program will help, nothing can come close to training hard and training right. As such, this is the most important step of the entire process. Fortunately for you, adhering to the principles-based training methodology introduced in Chapter 5 will ensure you adhere to the principles of muscle growth. But before you start making tons of gains, there are some loose strands that we must tie up.

Although I have provided you with a baseline weekly training volume, you may be wondering whether all sets will count towards volume. The answer is *NO*. As specified in Chapter 8, only hard, high intensity sets will count towards volume. This means warm up sets will not count towards your volume, mainly because the purpose of warm up sets is to warm you up – not stimulate muscle growth. Thus, when I specify "5 sets" for an exercise or muscle group, I am referring to 5 *working* sets.

So how should you tackle your working sets? Like many other training *methods* out there, how you tackle your working sets won't matter too much if you take your sets to failure. Whether you attack your sets with a pyramid approach, going from light to heavier loads and then back down, or an ascending approaching, where the loads used for each subsequent set is increased, is up to you. Likewise, the exact loads are up to you too. That's because, if you train with high intensity while adhering to the principle of specificity, you can stimulate muscle growth with *any* load – as elaborated on in Chapter 9. If you'd like to know more about the various training methods you can employ, go to www.andyxiong.com/bonus/hypertrophy.

If you're now thinking that building muscle is a really simple process, you'd be right. It was never complicated in the first place. Look at any successful bodybuilding program and you will notice that they have very similar volume ranges and exercises. However, depending on what muscle building program you look at, you might realize that there's an added complexity to their programming – in the form of periodization.

Periodization is a programming tool used to predict and direct training patterns, but if you've read Chapter 10, you'd realize that periodization is completely unnecessary for muscle growth. If you are a strength athlete you may need periodization, but if your goal is to build muscle the various periodization strategies might as well be marketing tools. Sure, periodization may let you use more complicated training techniques like overreaching or help you avoid overtraining, but none of these really matter when your goal is *only* muscle growth.

If you are still not convinced that periodization is unnecessary, I go more in depth on periodization, overtraining, overreaching and various other volume standards in *Bodyweight Workouts: How to Program for Fast Muscle Growth using Calisthenics Hypertrophy Training*. But training and building muscle is only as complicated as you want it to be; and truth is training hard and training correctly will make up the bulk of your gains. While others spend time trying to pinpoint nitty-gritty details like periodization, you can spend your time outworking them. And while they get pulled in different directions based on what different research-based "experts" claim (Chapter 2), you can train confidently knowing that all you need to do is adhere to the principles of muscle growth. The result? A bigger, more muscular, more confident and better you – someone who knows what you want, is confident that you can get it, and puts in the work to get the results that you want. That's the purpose of fitness and self-development after all: To become a more confident and better version of you.

References

Note: You can get a (clickable) PDF/printout of the references and more (such as an enlarged printout of free program) at www.andyxiong.com/bonus/hypertrophy.

Introduction

1. Midgley, Ben. *The Six Reasons the Fitness Industry Is Booming*. Forbes. 2018 Sep 26.
2. Patterson SD, Hughes L, Warmington S, Burr J, Scott BR, Owens J, Abe T, Nielsen JL, Libardi CA, Laurentino G, Neto GR, Brandner C, Martin-Hernandez J, Loenneke J. *Blood Flow Restriction Exercise: Considerations of Methodology, Application, and Safety*. Front Physiol. 2019 May 15;10:533.

Chapter 1: The Shockingly Simple Truth on How to Build Muscle

1. Barbosa-Netto, S, d'Acelino-e-Porto, OS, Almeida, MB. *Self-Selected Resistance*

Exercise Load: Implications for Research and Prescription. J Strength Cond Res. 2017 Nov 1.

Chapter 2: Introduction to Science, Evidence and Practice, and How to Tell Good Research from Bad

1. Fenton TR, Huang T. *Systematic review of the association between dietary acid load, alkaline water and cancer*. BMJ Open. 2016 Jun 13;6(6):e010438.

Chapter 3: The Science Behind Muscle Hypertrophy and Why Muscle Hypertrophy is Important

1. Nuckols, Greg. *The Complete Strength Training Guide*. Stronger by Science.
2. Johnson MA, Polgar J, Weightman D, Appleton D. *Data on the distribution of fibre types in thirty-six human muscles. An autopsy study*. J Neurol Sci. 1973 Jan;18(1):111-29.

Chapter 4: The Science Behind Muscle Hyperplasia and the Principles Behind Inter-Set Stretching

1. Kelley, G. *Mechanical overload and skeletal muscle fiber hyperplasia: a meta-analysis*. J Appl Physiol (1985). 1996 Oct;81(4):1584-8.

2. Evangelista, AL, De Souza, EO, Moreira, DCB, Alonso, AC, Teixeira, CVLS, Wadhi, T, Rauch, J, Bocalini, DS, Pereira, PEDA, and Greve, JMDA. *Interset Stretching vs. Traditional Strength Training: Effects on Muscle Strength and Size in Untrained Individuals*. J Strength Cond Res. 2019 Jul;33 Suppl 1:S159-S166.

3. Russ, DW. *Active and passive tension interact to promote Akt signaling with muscle contraction*. Med Sci Sports Exerc. 2008 Jan;40(1):88-95.

Chapter 5: Principles-Based Training Method, Backed by Science

1. Snyder BJ, Fry WR. *Effect of verbal instruction on muscle activity during the bench press exercise*. J Strength Cond Res. 2012 Sep;26(9):2394-400.

2. Loshe KR, Sherwood DE, Healy AF. *Neuromuscular effects of shifting the focus of attention in a simple force production task*. J Mot Behav. 2011;43(2):173-84. Wulf G, Dufek JS, Lozano L, Pettigrew C. *Increased jump height and reduced EMG*

activity with an external focus. Hum Mov Sci. 2010 Jun;29(3):440-8.

3. Marchant DC, Greig M, Scott C. *Attentional focusing instructions influence force production and muscular activity during isokinetic elbow flexions*. J Strength Cond Res. 2009 Nov;23(8):2358-66.

Chapter 6: The Science Behind Training Frequency

1. Schoenfeld BJ, Ogborn D, Krieger JW. *Effects of Resistance Training Frequency on Measures of Muscle Hypertrophy: A Systematic Review and Meta-Analysis*. Sports Med. 2016 Nov;46(11):1689-1697.

2. Yang Y, Bay PB, Wang YR, Huang J, Teo HWJ, Goh J. *Effects of Consecutive Versus Non-consecutive Days of Resistance Training on Strength, Body Composition, and Red Blood Cells*. Front Physiol. 2018 Jun 18;9:725.

Chapter 7: The Science Behind Rep Ranges and the Principles Behind Exercise Selection

1. Schoenfeld, BJ, Grgic, J, Ogborn, D, Krieger, JW. *Strength and Hypertrophy Adaptations Between Low- vs. High-Load Resistance*

Training: A Systematic Review and Meta-analysis. J Strength Cond Res. 2017 Dec;31(12):3508-3523.
2. Nóbrega, SR, Ugrinowitsch, C, Pintanel, L, Barcelos, C, and Libardi, CA. *Effect of Resistance Training to Muscle Failure vs. Volitional Interruption at High- and Low-Intensities on Muscle Mass and Strength*. J Strength Cond Res. 2018 Jan;32(1):162-169.
3. Schoenfeld BJ, Peterson MD, Ogborn D, Contreras B, Sonmez GT. *Effects of Low- vs. High-Load Resistance Training on Muscle Strength and Hypertrophy in Well-Trained Men*. J Strength Cond Res. 2015 Oct;29(10):2954-63.
4. Fisher J, Steele J, Smith D. *Evidence-Based Resistance Training Recommendations for Muscular Hypertrophy*. Medicina Sportiva. 2013 Dec;17(4):217-235.
5. Nuckols, Greg. *The Complete Strength Training Guide*. Stronger by Science.
6. Davies T, Orr R, Halaki M, Hackett D. *Effect of Training Leading to Repetition Failure on Muscular Strength: A Systematic Review and*

Meta-Analysis. Sports Med. 2016 Apr;46(4):487-502.
7. Damas F, Angleri V, Phillips SM, Witard OC, Ugrinowitsch C, Santanielo N, Soligon SD, Costa LAR, Lixandrão ME, Conceição MS, Libardi CA. *Myofibrillar protein synthesis and muscle hypertrophy individualized responses to systematically changing resistance training variables in trained young men*. J Appl Physiol (1985). 2019 Sep 1;127(3):806-815.
8. Staley, Charles. *P90X and Muscle Confusion: The Truth*. T Nation. 2014 Apr 4.
9. Rauch JT, Ugrinowitsch C, Barakat CI, Alvarez MR, Brummert DL, Aube DW, Barsuhn AS, Hayes D, Tricoli V, De Souza EO. *Auto-regulated exercise selection training regimen produces small increases in lean body mass and maximal strength adaptations in strength-trained individuals*. J Strength Cond Res. 2017 Oct 7.
10. Schoenfeld BJ, Ogborn DI, Krieger JW. *Effect of repetition duration during resistance training on muscle hypertrophy: a systematic*

review and meta-analysis. Sports Med. 2015 Apr;45(4):577-85.

Chapter 8: The Science Behind Training Volume, Sets and Rest Intervals

1. Jones, Nathan. *The New Approach to Training Volume*. Stronger by Science. 2015 May 12.
2. Baz-Valle, E, Fontes-Villalba, M, Santos-Concejero, J. *Total Number of Sets as a Training Volume Quantification Method for Muscle Hypertrophy: A Systematic Review*. J Strength Cond Res. 2018 Jul 30.
3. Schoenfeld BJ, Ogborn D, Krieger JW. *Dose-response relationship between weekly resistance training volume and increases in muscle mass: A systematic review and meta-analysis*. J Sports Sci. 2017 Jun;35(11):1073-1082.
4. Radaelli R, Fleck SJ, Leite T, Leite RD, Pinto RS, Fernandes L, Simão R. *Dose-response of 1, 3, and 5 sets of resistance exercise on strength, local muscular endurance, and hypertrophy*. J Strength Cond Res. 2015 May;29(5):1349-58.

5. Schoenfeld BJ, Contreras B, Krieger J, Grgic J, Delcastillo K, Belliard R, Alto A. *Resistance Training Volume Enhances Muscle Hypertrophy but Not Strength in Trained Men*. Med Sci Sports Exerc. 2019 Jan;51(1):94-103.

6. Haun CT, Vann CG, Mobley CB, Roberson PA, Osburn SC, Holmes HM, Mumford PM, Romero MA, Young KC, Moon JR, Gladden LB, Arnold RD, Israetel MA, Kirby AN, Roberts MD. *Effects of Graded Whey Supplementation During Extreme-Volume Resistance Training*. Front Nutr. 2018 Sep 11;5:84.

7. Amirthalingam, T, Mavros, Y, Wilson, GC, Clarke, JL, Mitchell, L, and Hackett, DA. *Effects of a Modified German Volume Training Program on Muscular Hypertrophy and Strength*. J Strength Cond Res. 2017 Nov;31(11):3109-3119.

8. La Scala Teixeira CV, Motoyama Y, de Azevedo PHSM, Evangelista AL, Steele J, Bocalini DS. *Effect of resistance training set volume on upper body muscle hypertrophy: are more*

sets really better than less?. Clin Physiol Funct Imaging. 2018 Sep;38(5):727-732.
9. Fisher J, Steele J, Smith D. *Evidence-Based Resistance Training Recommendations for Muscular Hypertrophy*. Medicina Sportiva. 2013 Dec;17(4):217-235.

Chapter 9: The Science and History of Intensity and Load

1. Lima BM, Amancio RS, Gonçalves DS, Koch AJ, Curty VM, Machado M. *Planned Load Reduction Versus Fixed Load: A Strategy to Reduce the Perception of Effort With Similar Improvements in Hypertrophy and Strength*. Int J Sports Physiol Perform. 2018 Oct 1;13(9):1164-1168.
2. Jones, Nathan. *The New Approach to Training Volume*. Stronger by Science. 2015 May 12.

Chapter 10: The Science Behind Periodization and How to Avoid Overtraining

1. Grgic, J., Lazinica, B., Mikulic, P., Schoenfeld, B. *Should resistance training programs aimed at muscular hypertrophy be*

periodized? A systematic review of periodized versus non-periodized approaches. Science & Sports. 2018 Jun;33(3):e97-e104.
2. Grgic J, Mikulic P, Podnar H, Pedisic Z. *Effects of linear and daily undulating periodized resistance training programs on measures of muscle hypertrophy: a systematic review and meta-analysis*. PeerJ. 2017 Aug 22;5:e3695.

Chapter 14: How to Tackle Plateaus and Stay Motivated

1. Muyor JM, Rodríguez-Ridao D, Martín-Fuentes I, Antequera-Vique JA. *Evaluation and comparison of electromyographic activity in bench press with feet on the ground and active hip flexion*. PLoS One. 2019 Jun 14;14(6):e0218209.
2. Bonnar D, Bartel K, Kakoschke N, Lang C. *Sleep Interventions Designed to Improve Athletic Performance and Recovery: A Systematic Review of Current Approaches*. Sports Med. 2018 Mar;48(3):683-703.
3. Helms ER, Zinn C, Rowlands DS, Brown SR. *A systematic review of dietary protein during caloric restriction in resistance trained lean*

athletes: a case for higher intakes. Int J Sport Nutr Exerc Metab. 2014 Apr;24(2):127-38.

4. Morton RW, Murphy KT, McKellar SR, Schoenfeld BJ, Henselmans M, Helms E, Aragon AA, Devries MC, Banfield L, Krieger JW, Phillips SM. *A systematic review, meta-analysis and meta-regression of the effect of protein supplementation on resistance training-induced gains in muscle mass and strength in healthy adults*. Br J Sports Med. 2018 Mar;52(6):376-384.

5. Mercimek-Mahmutoglu S, Salomons GS. *Creatine Deficiency Syndromes*. Gene Reviews. 2009 Jan 15.

Chapter 16: Push Muscles – Training the Chest, Triceps and Anterior Deltoids

1. Goto, M, Chikako, M, Hirayama, T, Terada, S, Nirengi, S, Kurosawa, Y, Nagano, A, and Hamaoka, T. *Partial Range of Motion Exercise Is Effective for Facilitating Muscle Hypertrophy and Function Through Sustained Intramuscular Hypoxia in Young Trained Men*. J Strength Cond Res. 2019 May;33(5):1286-1294.

2. Israetel, Mike. *Front Delt Training Tips for Hypertrophy*. Renaissance Periodization. 2017 Feb 06.
3. Pendlay, Glenn. *A Training System for Beginning Olympic Weightlifters*. Pendlay. 2010 Nov 11.

Chapter 17: Pull Muscles – Training the Upper Back, Biceps and Posterior Deltoids

1. Beardsley, Chris. *How should we train the trapezius?*. Medium. 2019 Jul 24.

Chapter 18: Leg Muscles – Training the Quads, Hamstrings, Glutes and Calves

1. Israetel, Mike. *Glute Training Tips for Hypertrophy*. Renaissance Periodization. 2017 Feb 14.
2. Contreras, Bret. *Dispelling the Glute Myth*. T Nation. 2009 Sep 16.

Chapter 19: Other Muscles – Training the Lateral Deltoids, Traps, Abs and Obliques

1. Israetel, Mike. *Trap Growth Training Tips*. Renaissance Periodization. 2017 Apr 17.

Printed in Great Britain
by Amazon